MW00652612

MUSIC PRODUCTION 2022+ EDITION

Everything You Need To Know About Producing Music, Studio Recording, Mixing, Mastering and Songwriting in 2022 & Beyond

TOMMY SWINDALI

DISCOVER "HOW TO FIND YOUR SOUND"

https://www.subscribepage.com/tsmusic

Scan the QR code for more.

Contents

MUSIC PRODUCTION, SONGWRITING, & AUDIO ENGINEERING, 2022+ EDITION: THE PROFESSIONAL GUIDE FOR MUSIC PRODUCERS, SONGWRITERS & AUDIO ENGINEERS IN MUSIC STUDIOS

MUSIC PRODUCTION FOR BEGINNERS 2022+ EDITION:

How to Produce Music, The Easy to Read Guide for Music Producers & Songwriters

INTRODUCTION

Welcome to Music Production for Beginners 2022 Edition! You may have been trying to find a way to take your artistic passions and turn them into a complete project you can release to the public, either as a hobby or as a prospective way of putting food on the table. This book will serve to walk you through not only the basics of music production but also how to get your music released on reputable platforms. You will learn things like how to make your music available to the masses as well.

Even for those with artistic talent who haven't received any formal training; this book starts right out the gate by filling in the gaps you may have in your knowledge, like industry-related jargon, sheet music reading, and even a few scales to practice helping teach you the basics of music theory.

Music is more than just an art form, it's also a discipline. If you hope to be successful at bending that artform to fill your pocketbook, you will need to practice discipline. You will also have to practice, practice, and yes, you will then have to practice, practice and practice. This cliche has been a cliche for a very long time despite its lack of originality, but if anything, that just serves to underline the truth it presents; the only way to grow as a musician is to push your limits. If you want to be successful in the music industry, you need to focus on the music and let it move through you, you need to take the time to know your music on an intimate level and find something transcendent about yourself that you can use as the building blocks of your artistic project. Once you have done this, you are ready to start down the road of professional music recording and production.

This book is a great tool for anyone with budget limitations, with tons of tips and tricks for minimizing production costs and even how to do things yourself that can easily save you thousands of dollars with practice. If you're new to music and want to learn how to record and produce music this is a great tool too! Even for younger artists, this can be a launchpad for you to explore your creativity. There may be a few words you need to ask an adult what they mean, or with adult supervision only, the internet can be a great place to find answers for the questions this book may raise for you.

A great way to cut costs on your music production is to learn how to engineer your own music. This book will explain some of the basics of music production and give you a platform to build off. If you know how to engineer your own tracks you don't have to pay for an audio engineer to record your session, which can be worth it, but quite costly! You'll also learn some of the most cost-efficient ways to set up your own recording space which saves even more money on not having to book studio time which can be inflexible and extremely costly over long periods of time.

There are hundreds of YouTube tutorials and online music schools that promise to teach you how to play or produce music. Without any direction, these platforms can make it difficult for beginners to create a solid basis of information to learn on. This book will help give you some direction in what you should focus on first with music, and then with production and other considerations for people looking to immerse themselves in the music industry. Using the knowledge from this book you can use YouTube and other online resources to fill any gaps and maybe you will see that you were approaching one idea or another from the wrong angle, and a shift of mentality can do wonders for your learning.

Even on days when you are busy, repetition and practice are incredibly important. Whether you do nothing but run scales absent-mindedly in front of the tv while dinner cooks, or write a verse every night before bed, make sure you are flexing those creative muscles every day. Not everything you create will be perfect, good, or even what you would consider music or art. However, art is subjective, and many of the most popular works of art were never even appreciated before the artist discarded them or packed them away to be found by someone else long after their death. It doesn't even matter if you make bad music every once in a while, as long as it's putting you on the path to something fulfilling and meaningful.

By taking the initiative to explore the wide world that is the creative industry, you are taking the first steps toward producing and releasing your own musical projects. The path

MUSIC PRODUCTION 2022+ EDITION

ahead of you is long, and there will be challenges and things that you struggle with. If you can manage to persevere you will come out the other side of this experience with a whole host of marketable skills that you can employ in your own music. This book contains a vast amount of information across a broad range of topics; take your time and take it in at your own pace. No matter the speed you progress with though, always make sure you are reinforcing your learning and experience with repetition.

Good luck!

CHAPTER 1

SONG INFORMATION

—————◄●O●►—————

Welcome to the beginning of your sound design journey! In this chapter, we will be starting with some music fundamentals by discussing terms like BPM (Beats Per Minute), Pitch, Frequency, and more concepts that are essential for you to understand before you begin to record, and even mix and master your music. Once we have the basics down, we will delve into what music genres are easy and affordable for beginner artists and producers to break into and start gaining experience.

Tackling these key points is essential to building a foundation you can build on! Even masters of the recording industry like

MUSIC PRODUCTION 2022+ EDITION

Kanye West, The Weeknd, and Daft Punk all started their journeys by mastering these basics, so let's get into it!

Beats Per Minute, Pitch, Frequency, and Other Jargon

The music industry and music theory, in general, has an ever shifting and growing number of phrases and terminology that are commonly used in the industry. This is called jargon. Every industry has its own jargon, it's like a special language that people with a shared industry, interest, or profession can use to communicate complicated ideas quickly. Some jargon comes and goes, but there are a few core terms that you need to understand inside and out before you start creating!

Tone is a piece of jargon that refers to the emotion that the music is trying to elicit from the listener; does the music make you want to dance? Does it make you want to cry? Shout into a pillow about your ex? All of that is because of tone!

Measures are made up of a set number of beats that usually remain consistent for most of, if not the entire, song. There are a set number of measures in each bar.

A *bar* is made up of several measures and can be used to create repetition or pacing in your music. It also serves to transition from one musical movement to another.

A *beat* is a term for how many notes can be played in each measure. Some notes span multiple beats, and others span only a fraction of a beat, this is another method artists can use to create diversity in their music.

Tempo is the speed at which each note inside a piece of music is played, creating overall pacing that always impacts the tone of the music.

Beats Per Minute (BPM), is all about how fast the music is playing. For example, when some families sing Happy Birthday, they sing quickly and with an upbeat tone, other families go at a much slower pace with more grandiose and purposeful singing. While both families are singing the same song, they are singing it at different BPMs. This is a common practice for musicians who use samples often, and for DJs to mix different songs together. Changing the BPM of a song can drastically change the tone the music emits.

Most music is made between 120 and 140 BPM, but other songs can have as little as 80 BPM. The term refers to how many beats will occur over the course of every minute of playtime. If you have an instrument, try playing some scales at a consistent pace, and then, doing your best to keep your pace consistent, increase the tempo. You have used rhythm and tempo to change the BPM you are playing scales at, and you will likely notice a very different tone that even simple scales can illustrate with this demo.

Pitch refers to the octave a note is played on. It is a common misconception that Pitch also refers to volume, however, this is simply because human ears are more sensitive to some frequency ranges than others. For example, you could play the middle C note on a piano, and then move an octave higher or lower on the piano and play the C note on that octave. The only difference between these two notes is the pitch at which it resonates. Go ahead and try this yourself on a keyboard or piano now, any instrument will work, but there are also many Digital Audio Workstations (DAWs) that you can access online and practice this concept with. More information can be found on DAWs when you reach Chapter 3: Studio Setup for Beginners.

Frequency is a concept that measures sound on a scale in a unit called Hertz (Hz). The human ear is capable of hearing between 20, and 20 thousand Hz, although hearing can diminish over the years, people can suffer hearing loss as well, and not everyone is born with the same ear canals, some humans can likely hear lower frequencies more distinctly than high ones and vice versa.

20 Hz is on the low end of human hearing, animals like whales are capable of hearing and producing frequencies much lower than this. For humans, this is close to the sound a 4-String Bass could achieve, (about 40-400 Hz).

Most humans are incapable of hearing higher than 18-thousand Hz because the higher end of the frequency spectrum is usually the first to become damaged over time or through enduring loud noises. In addition, the 16,000 Hz frequency range is unpleasant to the human ear, and in most cases, artists remove some or all these frequencies from their recorded music in the production stage.

Armed with the knowledge of this basic jargon you are ready to take the next step in your sound design journey!

Genres

Quite often budding producers, musicians, and artists face one major obstacle in their journey to creating music; money. The equipment, the services, and the professionals you will need to hire along the way can be quite expensive! In this section, you will learn about how to determine the best genres for new artists to break into based on startup costs and your individual musical interest and talent.

Electronic Music (EDM) is easily one of the cheapest types of music to learn how to make. There is a nearly endless supply of YouTube tutorials to help you learn how to make music on DAWs, or physical mixing decks, depending on your production style. Artists with an exceptional ear for pitch and a strong sense of rhythm are well suited to the EDM genre. With experimentation, repetition, and collaboration you can create beautiful and enthralling music with your own creative spin.

While there are many DAWs out there that are free or offer longstanding free trials like the Ableton 90-day-trial, which is a great option for someone who wants to make sure the program is right before making a purchase. Often free software workstations lack full support or functionality, and additional purchases may need to be made eventually to add functionality if the program is something that works for you.

The cost of EDM music can vary drastically to create. Production costs fluctuate based on things like how many tracks you would like to have active simultaneously, what instruments you would like available to you, whether you purchase samples, find free sources, or make your own samples all have varying degrees of cost, all of which will be covered in later chapters in more detail.

Hip-Hop, similarly to EDM can be created with free/cheap DAW software and usually vocals, aside from that there are many YouTube videos available to help you learn how to use DAWs just like with EDM. Artists with a strong sense of rhythm and creativity are well suited to Hip-Hop, sometimes being skilled at writing lyrical verse can also be an asset, but it is not necessary.

Hip-Hop relies on samples far more than EDM does, and quite often samples are used to create the melody and interesting audio effects with more organic instruments than EDM. Many Hip-Hop artists sample older songs from other genres like pop or Rhythm and Blues, partly to tap into a source of nostalgia that lends itself to the tone of the song, and partly because older songs do not need to be paid royalties when they are being sampled. 50-75 years (depending on the country) after an artist's death, their music becomes public domain and is available to be sampled freely.

Rap is one of the least expensive forms of music to create. The genre began as a form of spoken word by eloquently spoken members of the African-American community who would deliver rhythmic sermons or spoken word pieces. These artists were referred to as MCs or Masters of Ceremonies, with roots stretching back to before the abolition of slavery. Many rap artists created their first songs as children on the playground with little or no music to accompany them. At times other people even beatbox or use other percussive methods to add another layer of musical depth and rhythm to the piece. Artists who are driven by a message with strong literary skills are well suited to this genre, Rhythm is also an essential instinct for rap artists to master.

As a result of rap's deep roots in African-American history, the largest hurdle artists wishing to break into this genre face is understanding the ever-evolving jargon and tone that is prevalent in the modern rap community. This can be done by listening to artists within the genre, the more local the better, and reading different blogs about your favorite artists. Writing skills are essential! Remember, word choice and delivery are quite often the basis rap songs are evaluated so this should be the focus of most artists breaking into this industry.

Rap and Hip-Hop can overlap and intersect so much that they can appear to be nearly the same genre. However, Rap differentiates itself from Hip-Hop because while you can incorporate Hip-Hop elements to diversify the musical tone of your pieces, the elements of rap that are essential to qualify a piece of music for the genre are not necessarily the same requirements that qualify a song as a Hip-Hop piece.

Acoustic/Folk are both on the higher end of the cost spectrum for the genres we will be discussing. This is because even inexpensive guitars can cost more than some beginner artists may be able to afford, coupled with at least two microphones, an amplifier, and maybe some pedals for looping. People who enjoy storytelling can make incredible folk and acoustic artists, acoustic music also lends itself to other genres well and the acoustic guitar can be an extremely diverse instrument. It follows that the artists who favor the instrument would be well suited to many different group environments.

You could record vocals on your phone in a pinch, or even by plugging your over-ear headphones into the microphone jack, then singing into the earmuffs, this gives a muted, authentic Lo-Fi tone to your music which can be an asset in the folk genre but to capture the true sonic range of your instrument and voice, you should have a good quality microphone and stand.

If folk is your genre of choice, you may find you need to purchase more instruments and equipment to support the additional roles. The more people and instruments that are required to create your music, the more expensive things will be. On the other hand, if there are other artists in your group hopefully, they will be able and willing to contribute to the costs of the group. Communication is key to any group environment but for a band looking to produce high-quality music, it is essential.

Rhythm and Blues is a genre that can be quite expensive to record depending on the song, but it's also quite possible to do with a good quality microphone and a DAW, incorporating drum kits, synthesizers, MIDI instruments. However, if you would like to use tracks with your own instruments it can get quite expensive in the Rhythm and Blues genre. Many of the classical instruments commonly used in Rhythm and Blues also require years of extensive and technical training for artists before they are ready to be recorded. Artists with an impeccable sense of rhythm and a melodic voice are best suited to Rhythm and Blues. Quite often some technical singing instruction can be an asset, but many singers are naturally talented, and practice is always the most important thing for these artists.

With the basics down pat and an idea of what genres might be interesting for you to begin creating, you are ready to move on to the next step of your music production journey.

CHAPTER 2

MUSIC THEORY

———————◆O◆———————

Theory is usually the most tedious part of learning

how to play music well. In this chapter, you are going to learn

how to break down some of the basics of music theory in a

digestible way, and why these basics are important for

beginner artists to learn. Always think back to the previous

chapter's terms, genres, and how your genre can influence

which techniques you end up employing.

Reading Music

When it comes to music theory there are two main ways of

reading music, there are tabs that are exceedingly helpful with

learning guitar and other instruments where finger position is key. Once you have a good understanding of tabs and all the different notes in an octave you should attempt to transition to sheet music. This will allow you to play more fluidly and give you the skills to pick up a piece of music and play it without hearing it and piecing it together by trial-and-error.

There are twelve notes in each octave, The notes are named A, B, C, D, E, F, and G. They are only seven notes, the other five are notes between each of the lettered notes except for between B and C, and between E and F. These notes are known as either sharp or flat notes depending on the key and the melody being played. This means that there is no B sharp, or C flat. There is also no E sharp or F flat, although F flat is a term sometimes used in parts of the musical community, it simply refers to E.

Tabs

No matter what instrument you play there are likely tabs to help you learn individual chords and notes. Guitar players most commonly refer to tabs to learn music, many amateur guitar players are incapable of reading sheet music but are perfectly capable of learning songs if they are provided with the tabs.

Tabs use finger positioning and diagrams to teach people proper form and technique. People who are visual learners may find that Tabs will be the easiest way to pick things up in the early stages. Ideally, you should look for tabs that show what the sheet music signature for the same notation looks like. That way when you have learned the tabs you can use the association between the tabs and your finger positioning to recall the sheet music notation, and you will already have a head start on our next section!

Sheet Music

Before you start to explore individual notation, we need to learn about some of the symbols on sheet music that aren't about notes. There can be a great deal more information available for musicians on sheet music than with Tabs, and song flow is easier to read. That's why even though Tabs can be a great way to learn, serious musicians must eventually pick up the skill of reading music.

The Staff is one of the most essential parts of a piece of sheet music. It is made up of five lines and four spaced between them. Each space and line coincide with each of the notes that aren't sharp or flat.

The Bass Clef is a short and curved symbol with a large dot that rests on the F note in the staff. This is important for referencing sheet music. Depending on whether the staff is in the bass or treble clef this changes where the notes rest on the staff. On the bass clef, this will always be the lower spectrum of notes to be played in a song. There are many pneumonic devices that you can use to memorize notation positions on the bass clef, you can even come up with your own! One pneumonic device you could use is: Green Bulls Don't Fight Anyone.; From the bottom line up, each word represents the corresponding note that rests on a line in the bass clef. A pneumonic device for the spaces could be: Anyone Can Eat Grass. Like the previous phrase, this pneumonic device corresponds each word to a space on the staff, ranging from lowest to highest in pitch.

The Treble Clef is a tall and ornately looped symbol. Like the sign for the bass clef, the treble clef has a large round dot in its design. This dot hangs a line below the lowest line on the staff and corresponds with the C note on the treble clef. The Treble Clef represents notes played on the higher end of the frequency spectrum. Like the Bass clef, there are many pneumonic devices you can use to memorize notation positions from bottom to top. For the lines, you could use: Every Good Boy Deserves Fudge. For the spaces, you could use Free Alien Composing Expo, although some people prefer the acronym FACE.

Notes

Now that you understand some of the basics of sheet music, you are ready to dive into different notations and what each part of the strange symbols means! There are different parts of a note like there are different parts of your body. Each part serves a specific purpose. *The Head*, for example, is the round dot that sits on specific locations on the staff and denotes both what note is being played, but also the duration of the note.

If a Note is Solid and attached to a straight tail the note should be played for a single beat. If the note is hollow and has a tail, play the note for two counts, if there is a dot on the opposite side of the head from the tail the note lasts for three beats, if the note has no tail it lasts for four beats.

The Tail that hangs off a note can hang toward the bottom of the staff if the note rests above the middle line. Below that point, the tail hangs downward. Finally, there can sometimes be a flag attached to the end of the tail. This tag means that the note only lasts half a beat. If there are two flags the note only lasts a quarter of a beat, and this notation is rarely used. If the tails of one-note are straight thick bars connecting it to another note, that means that each set of the notes connected by the flags lasts the duration of a beat. For example, four notes which are *Beamed* together are notes played individually of each other but playing them takes the same amount of time it would take to play a single beat.

Sometimes a semicircle connects two notes in different measures. This indicates that the note should be held from one measure into another; this is called a *tie*.

Great! Now, go over this passage a couple of times, there's a lot of information in these short paragraphs, but with repetition and study, the images on a piece of sheet music will be simple to read and you will be able to use your new skill to effortlessly float through a piece of music. This can be a huge asset for artists looking to become session musicians, as being able to read sheet music and play an accurate replication of the desired song with little to no practice is a valuable skill.

Rests

There are five different types of rest notes. Two of the most common are relatively simple to identify. A *Whole Rest usually* lasts the duration of four beats and indicates a total lack of sound from the instrument or musician for the duration of that measure. The symbol is a small rectangular box hanging just below the middle line of the staff. *A Half Rest* lasts the duration of two beats and indicates the same lack of sound as the full rest. The next most common rest you will see in sheet music is *A Quarter Rest*. The symbol is a narrow vertical squiggly line that bows sharply in the lower half.

An Eighth Rest has a small head, with a curved tail that dips sharply past the head of the note before connecting to it. Finally, the *Sixteenth Rest* looks the same as an eighth rest, but there are two small heads connected to the tail.

Scales

Scales are one of the first things any great musician learns to practice. Dedicated artists practice every day if they have the time. Whenever you pick up your instrument or load up your DAW, run your instruments through a series of scales to help warm up your fine motor skills and get the creative juices flowing, not to mention warming up your ear.

A scale is a series of notes played within an octave, or sometimes, across a set of octaves in a rising and falling formation. Take care not to rush your scales and focus on rhythm and tempo while you practice so that you can work on those two essential skills to nearly every musical genre. Doing two minutes of dedicated scales every day is essential for fledgling artists to develop their ears as well, with enough practice, you should be able to identify what note another artist is playing on their instrument based on your own experience with scales, and then especially talented musicians can learn to emulate those notes and recite it back on their own instrument based off of their own ear.

The Piano is the easiest instrument to use to learn different notes and scales, but any instrument can be used. Notes are divided between half steps and whole steps between tones. This means that between notes C and D there is a half-step which is called both C Sharp, and D Flat, with the exception that there are no half step notes between notes B and C, or E and F. You will learn more about notes and how to read music in the second half of this chapter. However, this will be important to keep in mind when we discuss the four basic scales you will need to master and all of their variations.

The Chromatic Scale

The Chromatic scale is made up entirely of half steps and is the most basic form of scale to learn. This exercise will help you familiarize yourself with each of the notes. If you say each note aloud as you play it you will learn your notes faster and be able to move on to the next step in your creative journey. If singing is part of your art, you should attempt to harmonize with each note as you say it, this will double as a sort of vocal exercise in addition to honing your rhythmic and memorization skills.

To play a chromatic scale start by finding and playing C, then C Sharp, D, D Sharp, E, F, F Sharp, G, G Sharp, A, A Sharp, B, C, and then play the notes in the reverse order, except when you recite the notes in descending tones begin by playing C, B, B Flat (this is the same note as A Sharp), congratulations! You have just played your first scale! Don't worry if it wasn't perfect, there's a reason why practice is one of the most common traits of a successful artist. Practice this scale for two minutes each day for two weeks and you will notice a huge improvement in your rhythm and note comprehension. You should continue to play these scales as part of your routine, but now you will work on the next scale you'll be practicing.

The Major Scale

The Major Scale begins on a different note from the chromatic scale. The Major scale is made up of five whole steps, and two half steps. Notice how the tone of the Major scale is more uplifting and can even be triumphant. Like the chromatic scales, recite each note aloud as you play it, feel free to harmonize with your vocals.

To play a Major Scale begin by playing D then, play a whole note higher in tone, E, another whole note to F Sharp, then a half note, to G, a whole note to A, another whole note to B, a whole note to C Sharp, and a Half note to D. Play the notes in descending order, and make sure to use the Flat equivalent of the note names as you go.

Once you have learned this scale, incorporate it into your daily practice routine. After you complete two sets of chromatic scales, play two minutes of major scales, then to finish your practice, play two more chromatic scales. This will keep you refreshed with your chromatic scale but also give you something new to keep things fresh in your mind. Complete this process for two weeks. With the Major scale mastered the next one should be easy as pie!

The Minor Scale

The Minor Scale, like the Major scale, begins and ends on a D note. The Minor scale has a very morose tone and can often be associated with a feeling of melancholy. Just like the two scales before, recite the notes as you play your scales.

Play a D note, then whole notes up play an E, then a half note to F, a whole note to G, a whole note to A, a half note to A Sharp, a whole note to C, and finally, a whole note to D. Play the scale in reverse order, making sure to mind the fact that Sharp notes are now Flat.

Now that you have a new scale in your arsenal your practice regimen should change once again! Play two sets of chromatic scales, followed by two sets of Major scales before beginning your daily two minutes of Minor scales. After you have finished practicing your minor scales play two more sets of major scales, followed by two more sets of chromatic scales. Now we will move on to the final variation of scales!

Interval Scales

Lastly, Interval Scales are a more advanced form of scale, in which you either repeat a scale for several octaves or play the notes of a scale in intervals. This exercise helps you develop tempo to a greater degree and improve your finger work. Like all the other scales before this, continue reciting the notes you play.

To play a chromatic interval scale begin on C, then two whole steps up in tone to E, two more whole steps to G, and two more whole steps to C. Repeat this pattern for two or three octaves in each direction, making sure to reverse direction when you reach the end of the scale. You can also couple this scale with one of your weaker scales. For example, you could play an Interval Minor Scale that spans two or even three octaves if you find there is a particular scale that needs more attention.

Now that you are a master of scales your daily practice doesn't stop! Begin with 30-seconds of chromatic scales, followed by 60-seconds of chromatic interval scales, 60-seconds of major scales, 30-Seconds of 3-octave major scales, end with 60-seconds of minor scales, 30-seconds of 3-octave minor scales, and finish of with one minute of whichever scales you would like.

28

CHAPTER 3

STUDIO SETUP FOR BEGINNERS

———————◆○◆———————

For many beginners, setting up a studio is daunting; and one of the most important factors when setting up a recording or mixing space can be managing the costs associated with purchasing the equipment and materials you will need. This chapter is going to guide you through some of the best ways to set up a functional and achievable studio for recording or mixing music. Finally, you will uncover some essential tips to keep in mind when choosing and preparing your studio space.

Equipment

First, we have to talk about the equipment that you will need to buy. This is where the majority of new recording artists will end up spending most of their money. Whether you are pursuing a career in hip-hop or folk music, there are vital tips and topics you need to educate yourself on within the pages beyond! The upfront costs are an investment, as when you complete your first project and begin your next one, you will already have the necessary equipment for your creative process.

Studio Monitors and Headphones

When people refer to studio monitors, they are referring to a type of speaker setup which at least features two speakers that are 6" in diameter minimum and should be accompanied by a subwoofer which is, ideally equipped with a tweeter; a smaller-looking speaker found in the chassis that is designed to emit high-frequency tones. Are studio monitors essential for mixing music? Not necessarily, but they are one of the most reliable pieces of equipment to gauge how your sound is coming along from a sound design aspect. They give you the ability to mix a song both for ambient room listening, but it also gives you something to build on when you experiment with your songs through other means of listening, like earbuds and over-ear headphones.

You can use over-ear headphones for in-depth editing that requires a lot of detail. Quite often these over-ear headphones are used to edit parts of the music that may not show up on another speaker's frequency curve. When looking for a pair of mixing headphones you want to investigate two main things. Firstly, do they have a full frequency range available? You should look for headphones that are capable of producing frequencies between 20-20,000 Hz. Secondly, you should look at something called the Frequency Response Curve (FRC). Headphones have their own EQs and limiters inside of them, that's how, for example, some headphones boast the 'best' bass quality. What this often means is that the headphones are EQed to exaggerate the bass frequencies of any song played through it. This can be great for commercial listening and recreation, but in a mixing scenario, these types of headphones will lead you to suppress or elevate parts of the song that would ruin the tone if played through any other type of speaker or headphone. Usually, you can find this information online by searching for the FRC of the specific model of headphones you are considering, sometimes it can be found on the case of the product, but the information isn't always easily available, you may have to do some digging. For Mixing and recording, you are looking for the flattest FRC.

This is also why you should always mix your song through multiple speakers and headphones, as many different ones as possible. Mixing with in-ear earbuds is also possible, but usually, they lack the detail and sonic range of more established speakers. That being said, you should always listen to your song on regular earbuds as a routine quality check, as that's likely how people are going to listen to your music the most!

Microphones

Depending on the type of music you are planning to create, you may not even need a microphone, and this is a good place to cut costs if that's the case, however, the vast majority of musicians need microphones in order to properly capture the range and tone of their instruments and creative ideas. People producing EDM or solo instrument recordings might find that this is an expense they don't need to delve into. First, you will explore some unconventional microphone options that may not work for an entire project but could be used to create emotion and tone in your music.

Vocals are one of the most subjective things to record. If you have classical training and a burning need to belt out ballads like Adele, you'll want to invest in some very specific microphones, but for creating samples or rap and hip-hop vocals you could use a phone microphone. It won't capture the range of your vocal abilities the way a true microphone could, but can lend itself to a low-fi, and vocally percussive tone. Meaning your hard consonants will be more impactful but expect a high amount of what is called 'noise' which is ambient room noises collected by the microphone. In nearly every case, recording on your phone should be a last resort. There are even a few inexpensive microphones that connect with your phone that would work much better in terms of quality.

The 'Headphone Microphone' is when you take a set of over-ear headphones and plug them into the microphone jack of your recording device, then sing into the earmuffs of the headphones to record your vocals. This is not a technique that should be used for the duration of an entire song, the quality and vocal range will be muddy, and if you are trying to display any true singing ability, this will not convey it. However, the warm tone and muted sounds of the Headphone Microphone might work for a background ad-lib, or to grab listeners' attention during the hook or before a drop.

Moving away from the relatively free options there are a nearly endless number of different microphones out there. We are going to explore some versatile options that can work for vocals and instruments, as well as a couple of specialty options for specific instruments and vocals. There are three different categories of microphones out there. Dynamic Microphones, Condenser Microphones, and Ribbon Microphones, and they can be found in either USB or XLR connections. XLR connections will usually elicit better quality and allow the option of analog recording, which means less digitized sound files and achieving a truer audio parity. USB connectors are almost always less expensive, however, so for musicians who will be using digital wavelengths, or looking to keep on a budget, this is a great option.

Dynamic microphones are one of the most commonly produced types of microphones and this is due to their durability. For musicians looking for a microphone that will last a long time, and perhaps even some travel wear and tear, Dynamic Microphones are a great choice. These can be used on drum kits, bass, and guitars without risking too much distortion. A great example of a versatile Dynamic Microphone is the Shure Beta 58, or the Shure PGA 58 which is a well-regarded, but lower-cost option.

Condenser Microphones are different from dynamic

microphones in that they have a diaphragm inside the recording head of the devices. The sound pressure caused by the reverberations of sound will produce an audio signal that is superior to the magnets of a dynamic microphone. An important note about condenser microphones is that you will likely require phantom power to operate them unless it uses batteries. (Note that if it uses batteries, phantom power can harm the device.) Keep in Mind that condenser microphones inherently require a bit more care and attention than dynamic microphones. Take care not to use it to capture the sounds of a drum kit or bass guitar, ideally, they should be used for vocals and acoustic guitars. Condenser Microphones are higher in price range so for musicians looking to purchase these, look for the Audio Technica AT2035 for an example of a good entry-level condenser microphone.

Ribbon Microphones are by far the most fragile of the three microphones. The diaphragm of a ribbon microphone is a thin piece of metal that excels at recording vocals and instruments which don't put out very much percussion. Whenever you consider using a ribbon microphone you should always use a pop filter. It's not unusual for ribbon microphones to start at nearly 500-dollars, so if you are looking at this style of microphone make sure you have the studio space to match it. Musicians who have spent years training their voices to be able to showcase their vocal range may love the warm, intimate tone that ribbon microphones provide.

Digital Audio Workstations (DAWs)

For newer artists, there are a number of DAWs that you should consider. Different programs will provide different amenities depending on the type of music you are going to create. For EDM artists, your workstation is where you should be prepared to spend most of your startup money. There are some free-to-cheap options as well but for the EDM and Hip-Hop artists out there, they may not provide the range of services you need from a DAW given your chosen genre. Different workstations prioritize different things, while some focus on sample databases or MIDI notes, others are complex synthesizers first or primarily used for taking recorded audio and processing/mixing it.

Ableton is a piece of software that has been in the recording industry for years. Favored initially by the EDM community for its versatility and user-friendly interface; Ableton has also thrived in the Hip-Hop community for ease of sampling and song arrangement. The software currently comes in three tiers: Live 11 Intro, Live 11 Standard, and Live 11 Suite. The intro tier is perfectly capable of performing most things a new artist needs to have at their fingertips. The software brings 16 MIDI tracks, 8 mono input/output channels, four software instruments, 5GB of Ableton sound packs, complete with 21 audio effects and 11 MIDI effects to diversify your sound. The software costs $99 USD and is available on a payment plan.

All-told the Intro tier should be adequate for most beginner artists' needs. However, some EDM and Hip-Hop songs can easily meet and exceed the need for more than 16 tracks allowing for diverse arrangements and complex sound profiles. In these situations, the Standard edition may be the perfect fit with unlimited MIDI tracks, 12 Send and Return tracks, and 256 mono audio Inputs/Outputs. This tier allows audio slicing which is essential for editing samples, and Audio to MIDI; a godsend to any Hip-Hop or EDM producer. The package is rounded out by two software instruments in addition to the four available in the Intro software, 10 GB of Ableton sound packs, 36 audio effects, and 13 MIDI effects The software costs $449 USD, and is also available on a payment plan, just like the Intro version. The additional software instruments are one of the main draws of this pack, giving you more control over the sound you want to create.

For producers looking to build their own complex MIDI

instruments and arpeggiators run through DAW-board processing plugins, Ableton offers a Max for Live feature as part of their Suite tier of software that makes all of this possible and also gives you access to the full range of the Ableton Live DAW capabilities. The top tier of Ableton Live also boasts 17 Software instruments, a whopping 70 GB of Ableton sound packs, 59 audio effects, and 15 MIDI effects. The top tier of Ableton Live costs $749 USD, and like the two other tiers, the Live 11 Suite is available on a payment plan.

Ableton is a longstanding DAW that has been a staple in the recording industry for over a decade. No matter what your needs, Ableton offers a solution to your software needs, and they have developed an accompanying tactile interface called Ableton Push to take small producers to the next level. This DAW should fill the needs of any budding EDM or Hip-Hop artist at a flat rate with regular updates and support.

FL Studio is a mixing-mastering DAW, but if you decide to splurge for more expensive packages, you will increase the versatility and ease of interface for your projects. FL Studio offers its software in four different editions; Fruity, Producer, Signature, and the All Plugins Edition.

The Fruity edition is the entry-level version of the DAW. With an opening offering of 83 Instruments and effects, this DAW is a viable option for people looking to work out their song arrangements and MIDI processing. The Fruity Package costs $99 USD.

The Producer package has a bit more meat on its bones though. Six more instruments and effects, audio recording capabilities, and Edison and New Time Audio Editors round out the Producer package and expanded playlist features, all for $199 USD.

The Signature Edition includes all of the features of the previous versions and ups the ante with a Newtone Audio Editor in addition to 6 more instruments and full video and visual production capabilities. This package is an interesting option for artists looking to edit music videos as well. The Signature package rings up at $299 USD.

Finally, the All Plugins Edition from FL studios offers their full range of products including all three audio editors, 107 instruments, and effects, and all features included in the previous three packages. Currently, the All Plugins edition costs $499 USD.

Pro Tools is a full-service DAW from Avid. The software is an industry standard for recording, producing, editing, mixing, and mastering music. Many professional studios use this DAW, so being familiar with it is important if you ever plan to book studio time without hiring an engineer.

Pro Tools is available in two versions, The base version and the Ultimate version, both of which are available for free on a trial basis. After the trial has ended, they offer the service on a monthly subscription basis.

For most novice artists, the base Pro Tools package contains plenty of utility with 256 audio tracks, 1,024 MIDI tracks, 512 Instrument tracks, 128 Aux input tracks for direct recording, a video track, for creating music videos and film scores, an unlimited number of Busses, over 120+ Plugins, 5.4 GB of Avid sound packs, the software allows you to record sound with a sample rate of 192 kHz, and 32-bit depth. For any musician, this software can be the perfect bridge between your music, and release day. This version of Pro Tools costs $29.99 USD per month, while it provides much more accessible to new users, the monthly subscription can eventually cost as much as top tier software packages from other developers, but the widespread industry support and consistent access to recording tools can be an underrated asset for budding recording artists.

With all of this to offer Pro Tools Ultimate doubles down on production value for artists looking to incorporate physical workstations into their recording process. Many recording studios use this version, so being familiar with its features can be an asset. There is still value to be gained from this edition if you don't have access to physical hardware though, with an astounding total of 2048 Mono/Stereo/Surround audio tracks, this version also allows 2048 voices whether you are using an HDX Hybrid Engine workstation or a non-HDX station. For HDX Classic users, there are 256 voices available per card. Arrange your music with access to 512 Aux input tracks and routing folder tracks, 64 video tracks for complex video editing. The monthly cost for this edition is $79.99 USD. This package is a great option for larger groups looking to invest in studio time, and gain access to more advanced editing options.

Pro Tools is an essential tool for artists looking to break into the mainstream music industry and gain access to professional recording studios and Software. Large bands might find this DAW essential to the group's success within their genre. EDM artists and Hip-Hop artists can make use of the platform's expansive MIDI capabilities. Pro Tools is easily one of the most all-inclusive DAWs on the market.

Reason has long been integrated to work in conjunction with Pro Tools as an external plugin. Reason has also developed a full-service recording and mixing DAW in addition to the innumerable combinations of instruments and combinations. Reason provides a monthly subscription service, and Reason+ is available for $19.99 USD/month, grants access to over 75 different instruments, devices, effects, and includes weekly sound packs and constantly updated software. This tool is indispensable for artists. Specifically, EDM and Hip-Hop producers will find the varied options for synthesizers and other instruments are unlike any other software on the market.

For consumers looking to take their craft to the next level, Reason 12 is a physical rig that is specially designed to work with Reason+ and also offers artists the option to employ combinators, which allow you to chain devices together and create more elaborate soundscapes. EDM producers who are serious about creating custom synthesizers might want to consider shelling out the extra cash once they can swing it! The rig and DAW cost $499 USD for the complete package.

Logic is a great choice for artists using Macs as their computer of choice. This DAW is available for a free trial that lasts for 90 days, which is plenty of time to decide if you want to invest in the software or not. When the free trial is over, the software is available for license at the cost of $199.99 USD. The upfront cost may be difficult for some artists to contend with, but the program may be worth saving those pennies for.

Studio One by PreSonus is a unique entry in the market of DAW software. Their services are available on a wide range of payment options. For artists looking for a basic mixing and song arrangement DAW, the Studio One Artist pack may be sufficient for your needs! The package includes unlimited tracks, FX channels and plugins, five virtual instruments, complemented by 27 Native FX Plugins, and a 20 GB sample and loop library. This package costs a one-time payment of $99.95 USD and is more than adequate to meet the needs of many EDM and Hip-Hop artists.

If you would like to write your own sheet music, whether you play guitar or piano, the Studio One Professional suite includes much of the same features as the Artist package, with even more Native FX Plugins, a Mix Engine FX Plugin, a Score Editor, Project Page, Show Page, and a 40 GB Sample and Loop library. The Professional Package costs four times as much as the artist pack, however, and musicians considering this package may also want to inform themselves on the PreSonus Sphere, which is an all-inclusive creation suite designed by Studio One and includes all of the features of Studio One Professional and much more including access to all new libraries and sounds, more Native FX plugins than ever before, and notation software, including access to instructor live streams to further your craft! Rounding out this package is a sample and loop library that exceeds 100 GB and is frequently added to. PreSonus Sphere is available monthly for $14.95 USD, or on a yearly subscription of $164.95 USD.

This software provides incredible value to artists in the Acoustic genre, or who are looking to create big orchestra sounds without the massive expenses associated with recording a live orchestra. For the value, this service could be an asset to any artist looking to start working on their music from home!

Production Tips

When you begin creating and mixing your music the space you record from can change the tone of your music, or even make it unusable due to background or room noise. Knowing how to set up an adequate studio space can mean the world for your original recordings. This section will focus on small studios and how to get yours off the ground for as little cash as possible!

Acoustic Treatment

Some rooms are inherently better for allowing soundwaves to reverberate in a clear and pleasing tone throughout the entire song. Other rooms are detrimental to the soundwaves and can be difficult for recording. Typically, if the room you were considering for your studio was an exact square, 10ft by 10ft by 10 ft, this room would make a terrible recording area because the soundwaves won't reflect back into the microphone which can cause audio feedback or flutter and render your recordings useless. If at all possible, you should find a rectangular room so that your soundwaves can be deflected away instead of reverberated.

If you can't help but use a square room you may want to invest in some bass traps for the corner and some professional acoustic treatment, DIY remedies can only provide so much help in a square environment, but this will increase your studio costs drastically. Acoustic treatment should be used sparingly, as it can really be a precise science, but there are many DIY options. Many artists purchase a type of insulation called Owens Corning 703. The material is very absorptive and can dissipate sound waves. Typically, the insulation is framed in 1x1 wood, and a canvas can be stretched over it to create a panel. As an added step if you know anyone handy with a paintbrush, this could be an opportunity to let the acoustic treatment contribute to the creative process of the musicians as well with personalized artwork that doubles as acoustic treatment. These panels should be placed above speakers to avoid muddying the sound, and in patches behind the workstation. In front of the artist, they should create some diffusers, which can be made simply by placing egg cartons on the wall but framing them with canvas like the insulation is a good way to help the treatment look more aesthetically pleasing, but more importantly will reflect soundwaves away from the flat surfaces and avoids unwanted reverberation.

For vocalists looking to record at home, you could sacrifice your closet and acoustically treat it with egg cartons from floor to ceiling as diffusers, (and on the ceiling too). Hang a microphone from a clothes hanger and you have an adequate space to record your ballads, dis tracks, or pop anthems.

Small Studio Setups

The trick with small studios is quite often, choices need to be made. Whether the limitation is space, money, or availability; starting a small studio where you can express yourself to the fullest comes with its fair share of challenges and responsibilities. One of the first things that artists need to realize is that maintaining their equipment will save them far more money than anything else they can do in the industry. Any computer you rely on for work should be cleaned properly with compressed air and cotton swabs. Dust will erode your electronics, so cleanliness is paramount in your studio space, particularly if you are using physical equipment and Plugins, Stock up on the disinfectant wipes!

Typically, a home studio setup will consist of a computer, which may be a desktop, or a laptop depending on whether you want to be able to take your creative process on the road. You will also need DAW software to go with that computer, of which there are many choices. You will require a set of headphones, and a pair of studio monitors if you can afford them, and any physical interface you want to add to your DAW's versatility, whether it's a MIDI keyboard, a drum pad, or a controller device. Some artists will need microphones and instruments to round out their first studio setup, and they are off to the races!

If you are trying to create a focused studio space, the first choices to be made are what pieces of equipment do you need to purchase? This is when a budget comes into play. Look at how much you have to spare for startup costs now and see if you can meet that budget in the planning phase. If your equipment will cost more, you can always buy what you can at the moment and save up for the rest, wait for sales, or purchase used or refurbished pieces! Your creativity will have to be an asset in more than just music to meet the goals you've set for yourself!

When you are first starting out, think about only what is essential, sometimes a solid condenser mic, your favorite DAW, and a bunch of egg cartons can be all you need to get off the ground and start getting your creative vision ready to present to the world. Some of the most inspired albums in history were born in the depths of a shadowy basement, but if your vision requires acoustic precision and outboard processing, then you can start exploring what processors might be worth purchasing. Even how to make your own acoustic treatment and choose the best software for you. Just be aware that this can quickly become costly and ineffective for your goals.

Being able to rent out any studio space you manage to create is a good way to recoup expenses and justify more expensive equipment and software, but this requires business savvy as well as creativity to run a studio business on the side. For groups that choose to record in a detached space like garages or sheds, this can be a great option, but be sure to take safety precautions and invest in an alarm system. Taking more expensive equipment offsite when it's not in use and at night can help reduce your risk of theft, and help you determine what equipment you use frequently, and what you might be able to sell to recoup some of the cost of the purchase. Remember, if you plan to rent a space out to artists, it must be clean, private, and equipped with the basic equipment necessary for projects you agree to take on.

CHAPTER 4

VIRTUAL STUDIO FX AND INSTRUMENTS

———————◆O◆———————

Now that you have your equipment, and your DAW of choice laid out, the next step in your mixing and mastering journey is learning about the different possibilities your workspace affords you. With the power of modern technology, music has broken free of the limits it has known in the past, and endless possibilities are waiting to be explored with your own unique brand of imagination. First, we will discuss Plugins; all the different variable affects you can choose to modify your audio files with. Plugins come in all shapes and sizes, but we will focus on Pitch, Reverb, Autotune, and Looping. After mastering the basics of these essential FX and Plugins you will learn about what synthesizers and MIDI are and what they mean for your music-making and creative

50

processes. This will give you everything you need to mix and create your music with the tone you desire.

Virtual Studio FX

Pitch

Many EDM and Hip-Hop artists will need to familiarize themselves with pitch bending functions on their software. Bending the pitch of the sound will change what octave on which the auditory range is played, although the note will not change. Changing the pitch of a C note, merely changes what octave the C note is played in, not the note itself.

This is useful to many artists who want to alter the tone of samples being used or string one melody into another seamlessly. With the creative application, pitch bending can make completely unique sounds from the original audio, and with practice, this technique can be used to combine multiple sounds.

Whether you are changing the pitch of a single note to draw the ears of your listeners before a big drop or lowering the pitch of a sample so that it sits perfectly in the background vocals while your own lyrics are recorded in the foreground;

changing pitch makes your music more diverse, and this technique can keep listeners learning new things about your project and bring them back for multiple listens. Experiment with it yourself and see how bending pitch can help your creative process in the digital age of recording.

Reverb

Reverb is used in almost every piece of music that is sonically treated. Reverb is the delay of soundwaves to create the impression of an echo. Reverb can be created in an analog way with the proper acoustic treatment and locale. For example, bathrooms tend to have very high amounts of natural reverb, and this is why singing in the shower sounds nicer than when you hear your own voice played back to you. The only drawback to natural reverb is that the materials that make up your surroundings; like the ceramic tiles of a bathroom- color your music. Too much reverb will make your music sound muddy and distant, but the right amount gives a tone of ethereal beauty or haunting sorrow. Reverb will help you bring emotion into your music, which is the root of all music in the first place!

Autotune

Autotune is a staple in the recording industry. Many artists, and even practiced vocalists use autotune. You can use this program to make your voice sound like Akon or Kanye from the early 2000s, of course, but you can also use it to fix small but significant falters in vocal performance, bringing a piece from impressive to exemplary.

There is a common misconception that Autotune is a magical plugin that instantly makes any artist's vocal performance sound flawless. In reality, overuse of autotune tends to result in dramatically pitch-bent notes or sometimes, if vocals sound too perfect the human ear will detect that there is some processing there. Even if your listeners don't have the technical know-how to put it into words, this will impact the perception of your music. If used properly, autotune can be used to correct minor missteps, making a note sharper or flatter, depending on the needs of the song, but be careful to leave just enough flaws that the performance sounds real and authentic.

For those still unconvinced that autotune is a legitimate effect to employ in your music, consider this; when you apply equalizers to your hi-hats to remove the unpleasant frequencies and latent room-noise, you are applying the same degree of processing to that hi-hat, that autotune can apply to a vocal performance. Yet the drummer's skill is seldom called into question because of this. Autotune is a legitimate Virtual FX plugin to invest in, and just like any other plugin; if it is used with skill and care, it will help you create the soundscapes you desire.

Looping

Looping has been used in nearly every genre to-date, and the technique predates digital processing and was one of the first analog processors to be developed. Looping can be used to great effect whether you use it to build a melody and beat piece by piece while your listeners bear witness, or just to continuously repeat that bassline with a unique tone.

Sometimes the audio sample that you are importing may be a different bpm than the track you're building. In this instance, you simply have to time-stretch the sample before looping. To do this, place your sample in the song arrangement on your DAW, and line up the beginning of the sample with the beat you want the sample to start on. Click and drag the right edge of the sample, until the BPM matches your current song, then you are ready to loop your new sample, and apply other effects to it.

Looping is one of the oldest tricks in the book, literally! Nearly any musician can find a use for this tool which is favored most by EDM and Hip-Hop artists who often rely on various samples to make up their songs. This tool will take your mixdown sessions to the next level and ensure consistent pacing and tone throughout the track.

Synthesizers and MIDI

For many artists, samples, Synthesizers, and MIDI instruments make up the majority of their tracks in the early stages of their recording careers. Even established artists and producers consistently rely on these tools. Samples will be discussed in Chapter Six, which is entirely devoted to finding, and creating samples. This section will focus on the other two components: Synths and MIDI instruments.

Synthesizers

Synthesizers come in many forms these days. There are innumerable virtual synthesizers available for purchase that provide artists with incredible processing power and versatility, and there are physical synthesizer plugins that can bring a warm, authentic tone to your music if used as a driving characteristic.

Synths are made up of various sound generators, oscillators, and filters to create complex sounds that can't be replicated by traditional instruments. They are a growing staple in the music industry spanning across genres, but many EDM artists rely on synthesizers to a unique degree when compared to other genres. For these artists, they may want to consider purchasing one or two physical plugins that you can route into your DAW software, but virtual synths work perfectly fine. Reason is now a full-service mixing software, but originally it was one of the foremost synth software on the market, and they have only built on that reputation. Reason plays well with other DAWs as long as you can run it through a ReWire plugin which provides the versatility to create your own synthesizers and audio processing effects that you can route into your DAW or audio project.

Synths can be useful in nearly any genre, but more than anyone else EDM and Hip-Hop artists thrive off of these versatile tone generators. Even for others, adding a synth tone in the background of your vocal track, or even the melody, can have a drastic shift on the impact your music can have on listeners.

MIDI Instruments

MIDI (Musical Instrument Digital Interface) is a piece of technology that came into popularity around the same time as Digital Recording. MIDI has many potential purposes, from controlling synthesizers and processing effects to laying foundation tracks that you can record over later when you know how you want to process the sound, that way if you end up spending money to hire studio time instead of creating your own recording setup, you will be organized and ready to focus on your creative process and putting out the music your listeners deserve and want to hear from you.

Musicians who want the most authentic-sounding MIDI instruments should look for polyphonic MIDI controllers which allow them to send multiple MIDI signals, (or individual notes making up a chord). Using these types of MIDI controllers, you can produce the most authentic sounds available, which is ideal if you are looking to use a MIDI controller and sampled instruments to create your music. Many artists use MIDI instruments in their finished products. The main thing to look out for if you want to use this technique is that your instrument samples are high-quality. This means low room noise, good finger position, and sometimes breath control in the original recorded sample. The fewer processing affects you put on a sample, the more authentic it will sound to your fans, and the better it will sound if you end up mastering your tracks. Look for more on mastering in Chapter 11, where you will learn the dos and don'ts of one of the audio mastering processes.

Some artists use MIDI notes to give them an idea of what their songs will sound like when they can record them live. This is a great idea for artists who play in large groups but do not have their own recording space. The audio engineer of the group can sub in MIDI samples for instruments you aren't able to record. This means when you go to a recording space or studio that you have to pay for, you are able to predict how things will sound when you have recorded them, and the musician can listen to the MIDI notes while they play to help with their own tempo, and tone. Classical composers or producers who work with large orchestras or bands will find this to be an essential asset, as paying for large bands to record can be extremely costly.

CHAPTER 5

INSTRUMENTS

————◀●▶————

Different Instruments elicit different tones and bring different emotions to your listener's mind that can be affected by the timbre (the natural sound) of the instrument. Quite often the natural sound of an instrument combined with a musician's unique style is something you want to capture with as much sonic detail as possible. There are many ways to ensure your instrument performs as well as possible in a recording. First, we will discuss some basic sound design tips and a few tricks for recording common instruments. Second, we will focus on the sound design of Bass guitar and drum sets, which are uniquely important sounds for the impactfulness and rhythm of the track.

Sound Design

Every instrument elicits its own tones and emotions and choosing what instruments to bring into your track is the first step of sound design. Maybe you'll have a synthesizer, a drum machine or kit, some vocals, and a guitar or piano for a melody. It is essential to have something to keep the rhythm and timing of the rest of the track, this usually falls to the bassline and drum sets, the vocals add a narrative depth to the song while the melody brings it home. In this example, the synth plays the role of the bassline, but it can just as easily be a part of the melody spending on what frequency is being synthesized.

Now that you have chosen your instruments you need to decide if you will be recording with high-quality MIDI samples or recording direct sound. Even if you choose direct sound, MIDI notes can stand in for your physical instruments until you get the chance to record the real deal!

Processing is the next thing you need to assess. Listen to each of your sounds individually and determine whether there is room noise or anything else you want to alter about the sound. From that point, you can add reverb, apply equalizers, or pitch bending, even looping the audio to create your desired sound.

Once you apply processing to a single sound, reference it back to the track at large and listen to the sound as part of the arrangement. Make any additional tweaks and continue on to the next tone! Before you know it, you will have assembled and processed your entire track and you'll be ready for the mixdown! More on that in Chapter 10!

Guitars

Of course, there are two overarching types of guitars you might need to mic up. One is acoustic, which can be effectively mic'd up with one or two microphones. One good quality condenser mic, although a dynamic mic could work if that is what is in your budget. The mic should be placed three-to-six inches from the soundhole of the guitar. This will pick up a great range of tones both from the instrument, and the recording environment itself. The second microphone in this setup is optional, and the levels on this track should be reduced and processed to couple with the first mic's input. The second mic only needs to be dynamic, and capable of recording the guitar's fretboard, which adds a very authentic tone to your guitar strumming. The microphone should be placed six inches from the fretboard and be sure to face the recording head of the microphone properly towards the fretboard to pick up the best directional sound.

With electric guitars, the mic setup can be drastically different. Sometimes the guitar will be plugged directly into the input of your recording software, instead of an amplifier. This is a great option as it allows the artist to hear their instrument being played in the mix in real-time without having to spend the extra cash on another microphone or worry about the logistical issues of micing up an amplifier. The main reason why you might want to mic up an amplifier is if you like the tone of the room you are recording in, or if the specific timbre of the instrument which you are trying to record can only be heard through the amplified tone. The fretboard could also be mic'd up for an electric guitar to give it a grittier, more present-sounding tone.

Pianos

Pianos are difficult instruments to properly mic up. First of all, they quite often require specialized acoustic treatment to record without worrying about echoing soundwaves off the walls. placing some diffusers outside of the piano's recording sphere can reduce room noise and echoes. You can use dynamic microphones to mic up a piano perfectly fine, but directional condenser microphones excel at recording pianos, due to their directional recording cone, and being able to catch the ambient tones and voice coming from the instrument. As many as five condenser mics should be placed in a semicircle around the body of the piano, angled toward the piano about five inches from the body of the piano. one dynamic mic could be hung above the piano to catch the ambient reverb if you want to try to apply that later.

Wind instruments

Recording with wind or brass instruments should be done in a quiet space, with as little ambient room noise as possible to interfere with the natural timbre of wind instruments. Sometimes a vocal booth would serve this purpose, sometimes you can just place large dampeners on all sides of the artist and recording setup, to minimize room noise. Usually, one condenser mic placed three to six inches from the mouth of the instrument will capture the sound clearly and without too much interference. Be sure to watch levels and make sure that there's no unintentional peaking.

Vocals

Recording vocals in your bathroom is probably not the best choice for most projects. Sure, the space has great reverb and there are some really great qualities that you can elicit with natural reverb, but the tiles tend to provide a type of acoustic treatment that can sound a little canned. Typically, you will need a vocal booth to properly treat the recording space for the vocal tracks. For ways to treat your own spaces for music look back to Chapter 3: Studio Setup for Beginners. Vocalists should stand about 5-6 Inches from the microphone. Depending on the type of singing you specialize in different mics might be ideal. Ribbon mics give a warm, and emotive tone to your music and are ideal for tracks where the vocals are at the forefront of the music. A pop filter should always be used as a layer of protection over the microphone. Ribbon Mics are very costly which means they should be handled with great care, especially if you try to use them outside of the studio. Some vocalists prefer to use condenser microphones because they can be vastly cheaper than Ribbon Mics, and their figure-eight recording pattern can be ideal for picking up traces of environmental noise in a live environment, but this can be completely controlled in the studio by using a vocal booth. This will add a slight natural reverb to the tone, and condenser mics are more durable than Ribbon Mics which makes them slightly easier to travel with although they should be handled with care if you plan to use them on the road; if the diaphragm is damaged the microphone won't be able to record properly. Finally, some vocalists who tend to travel for gigs might opt for dynamic mics, they can handle the stress and strain that live audience and percussive sound waves put on the mic. Ribbon mics can easily be damaged in this environment and even condenser mics can be damaged by heavy percussion but should hold up fine for the most part as long as you don't place it too close to the drumset.

Bass and Drums

When musicians are playing in a group, the bass guitarist and drummer drive the rhythm and tempo of the music, if the drummer or bassist is off, everyone is off. That's why it's so important that you know how to properly record these instruments.

The bass guitar should be recorded through Direct Input if possible because the sound is then played back into the headphones of each of the recording artists so they can hear how they sound as they are being recorded. The clearer sound brings a sense of rhythm and tempo for other artists to take their cues from, and to bring the audience into the beat of the track.

You should also consider putting a microphone on the fretboard to get some ambient noise and finger movement sounds. For these purposes, a dynamic mic will work perfectly.

Micing up a drum kit is one of the most complex parts of recording a musician. Using a wide range of dynamic microphones with specific placements you will be able to record crisp, clean drum sounds and authentic drum loops without employing MIDI technology. MIDI is an incredible tool, but there is nothing that can replace the natural rhythm and tone of a drum kit which you can tune at a moment's notice for changes in timbre. When playing in groups, having a drummer to drive the beat is much more effective than listening to a MIDI track of drums via headphones, even if it is recorded at the same time.

A drum kit is usually made up of a Kick, snare, hi-hat, cymbals, low toms, and high toms. A lot is going on here and recording these pieces is precise art! Keep in mind that in live performances there are different miking techniques you may want to employ, but we will focus on the recording environment.

When recording in the studio, any damping mechanisms that are built into the drums should be removed, as they tend to increase rattling. Instead, you should try covering the drum kit with a towel or placing a wallet on the drum and striking the wallet to dampen the blow.

Kick

The most percussive piece of the drum set, and the keeper of the beat, micing up a kick is very important to the overall sound of the track. The kick puts out the lowest frequency tones and brings a punchy quality to the track. A dynamic mic is the best option for this instrument as it can handle the high sound pressure levels that it puts out. and a large-diaphragm mic is ideal because it causes a base boost due to the directional recording pattern of the microphone. Experiment with the distance of the microphone, as different distances will change the tone. Placing the microphone closer to the instrument will give the sound a more impactful low end, which is a sound common in Hip-Hop and Rap for their forceful rhythm. When you move the mic farther from the sound source it will give the kick a sharper tone with more high frequencies. These techniques can be popular for EDM tracks. Experimentation is your friend in this case. Move the mic to a few different locations and fine-tune your sound. The less processing you can put on your recorded sounds, the cleaner your finished product will sound.

Toms

Depending on your resources or artistic choices, you can

choose to mic your Toms individually, or in sets, (Hi and Low Toms). When miking Toms one at a time, you should place your microphone about an inch from the outer rim of the instrument, maybe two inches to achieve a pure tone without any other bleeding from nearby instruments. As far as three to six inches from the rim of the drums gives a more high-frequency tone. Using a microphone with a cardioid (heart-shaped) recording pattern is best, and you can place it in between the two drums so that each side of the cardioid recording pattern will capture each Tom. Sometimes, you may want to try removing the bottom of the toms and placing a cardioid mic inside of the drum, about 1-6 inches from the top of the drum. This technique gives your music a bassy tone with less attack.

Snare

Snares are known for their punchy sound. To achieve this, you should start by taking a dynamic mic and placing it about one inch from the inside of the top rim. Take care to leave the Hi-Hat and rack toms in the mic's blindspot so that you can avoid these from bleeding into the track. If you want crisp and light snare tones, place a second cardioid mic underneath the snare. When recording, reverse the polarity on the recording of the lower microphone and combine your two Snare mics into a single track to get the full drum sound. If you opt for this technique you may want to try to find some super-cardioid mics, which will have a much tighter recording pattern and minimize sonic bleed.

Hi-Hat

Hi-Hats produce a high-frequency tone that can be captured from many angles to achieve different things. Feel free to experiment and find a setup that works for you. Placing the mic above the instrument will allow you to capture a sharper sound including the sound of the drumstick striking the top. You can place the mic on the bottom if you are looking for a flatter-toned high-frequency.

Cymbals

Quite often referred to as the 'Overheads' there are usually two mics responsible for capturing the sounds of the Cymbals and the rest of the kit to a lesser extent. Condenser mics are ideal for this type of recording due to their ability to reliably capture high frequencies produced by Cymbals. The mics should be placed on either side of the Cymbal array and should each be the same distance from the kit to ensure the sonic fidelity of your track.

CHAPTER 6

SAMPLES

Many of you may have heard part of an old song from the '60s, or a videogame soundbite, an excerpt from a TV show, or political stump speech spliced into your favorite songs and processed or looped in order to ridicule or underline the original audio. Many of these audio samples become cornerstone identifiers and trademarks for the artist who adopts them. Many producers covet their sample collections as they are the most important tool in their repertoire. In this chapter, we will discuss how you can find the highest quality samples available, whether they can be found on the internet through a subscription, or a free service. Even creating your own samples from the world around you is a great way to tie your creativity to the parts of your life that inspire you. The artists who can use their samples to set themselves apart from the rest of the industry, they will find their fans feel closer to the message of the music and it will give them a repeatable and predictable phrase to draw the attention of listeners.

How to Find New Samples

There are already so many great sounds and recording artists who have taken good quality samples all across the world and have made them available via the internet. Why reinvents the wheel? The old traditions of MCs flocking to vinyl stores to find their next sample in the warm supple tones of analog recordings have fallen by the wayside somewhat but there are still those who use the same method today to great effect.

Free Samples

For those who have little spending capital to devote to finding samples, there are many free options for you to explore, but you may have to search through more on free sample sites in order to find that diamond in the rough that suits your project perfectly.

One of the most renowned free sample sites is Zapsplat with nearly 100,000 different samples included in their library.

The sounds featured in their library range from animal and nature sounds to music, foley, and ambient noises. These samples quite often have dozens, or in some cases even hundreds of options in each category so that you can find your perfect sample!

Looperman is another free sample service where samples are uploaded by artists and producers just like yourself! Eventually, maybe you will even contribute to the community! At the time of publication, the website boasts a staggering 190,000 audio sample library of user recorded audio at your fingertips, and the library grows every day. Communities coming together to provide free and easily accessible samples for other musicians or producers is an incredible testament to the human desire to collaborate creatively. Seizing this opportunity can mean combing through hundreds of audio loops to find one that meets your audio quality and production specifications. Whether you are looking to find audio of classical instruments or more contemporary tools of the trade, Looperman is a massive library of free musical samples.

Sampleradar is a free sampling service offered by MusicRadar. The service boasts more than 73,000 downloads and those aren't individual sounds. Each download is a sample pack that MusicRadar adds to the collection regularly. The sounds range from individual instrument tracks to ensemble samples, and ambient noises.

Sample Subscriptions

Sample subscriptions can be found primarily in two forms. One is as a website or service devoted entirely to the production and release of high-quality audio samples for use in your next project. Some DAW subscriptions are discussed in Chapter 3: Studio Setup for Beginners, which includes sound library subscriptions that will be added to your library. For those looking for the widest possible range of samples, you should keep an eye on the offerings from your own preferred DAW program until you have a library large enough to have multiple usable sample options for any given sound you may want to access.

Splice is one of the most respected paid sampling services. They have added a substantial portion of the Converse sound library to their offering of samples. They offer variations of One-shots, FX, MIDI, and presets. The service is a monthly subscription so you can access any of the sounds in the library individually if you don't want to download unnecessary files that you don't plan to use or will have to clean out later. This option is much more hard drive-friendly than the average method of downloading sample packs. You can import the RAW files directly into your DAW platform. Their curated catalog of samples can be searched using similar sounds to help you find the perfect version of your particular sample.

Some services like Cymatics combine both approaches by offering both free sample packs and paid audio packs for those who require premium recordings. This can sometimes result in better recordings being locked away until you decide to shell out the cash for it. Cymatics offer loops ranging from melody stems to drum loops and plugins. You can even find a selection of one-shots and MIDI notes as well. Currently, the service offers over 100 free and paid samples for artists to access.

Making Your Own Samples

Making your own samples can require some specialized equipment to pull off. Some solutions can be as simple as purchasing a decent condenser mic, a laptop complete with your favorite DAW software, and a recording interface. You can find used interfaces that work perfectly fine if you are short on resources. You should also have a pair of over-ear headphones for you to inspect your samples on playback. This allows you to tweak your technique if the original recording doesn't meet the standards you have set for them. Like anything in music practice and repetition will pave the way to success and driven by your passion you can achieve some truly unique ideas within the music industry.

Now that you've gathered your equipment, there are three main branches of sounds we'll cover that are readily available for artists to incorporate into their art. Ambient noise is a good thing to throw into the background of a track or signify a change in tempo, even punctuating a key thought or musical movement the track is based on. Personal epithets or interviews with loved ones can be used to a high degree with a little production value. Finally, the samples that might be most magical as editions to your music are the found sounds, like the natural noises of the city, or the song of a bird.

Ambient Noise

Ambient noise refers to the sounds that your given environment creates just by existing. This can mean recording the crickets as they chirp at sunset, or something as simple as positioning a condenser mic three feet away from an oscillating fan in an empty room. Ambient noise is an abstract concept that can help you stretch the limits of your imagination and truly grow as an artist. There's an undeniable structure to the beauty the world around us offers. The art of sampling ambient noise depends on your ability to hear the beautiful sounds around you and isolate them in the recording. Ambient noise doesn't require precise miking techniques, but like everything in this industry, the only way to find the limit of your potential is to practice and expand on what you've learned every time you create.

Personal Interludes

Interludes have been a tried-and-true tool within the music industry for decades now. Whether you want each verse to be punctuated by an excerpt of your own monolog or a conversation with someone you respect. Really, it all depends on the type of tone you are trying to emit with your samples. Sometimes arguments are a popular thing to use in the background of your track, whether real or fabricated. Beware, if you expose personal conversations based on high-tensions and emotions in your music, others may not like what you have to say if they were involved in the recorded sample. Be ready for the fallout of this particular use of sampling and remember that it's always best to obtain consent from anyone you want to sample for your music.

This can become difficult if you are attempting to sample the speech of a public figure or celebrity but attempting to contact them for permission may be worth a shot!

Found Sounds

There are so many ways to punctuate the movement in your track, not least of which is the quirky sounds you can record. To many, this is known as Foley, and there is a wide range of existing recordings to access but if you have specific sonic requirements for your project you may want to record your own samples because of equipment, environment, or timbre of the recorded sound. The sound of glass breaking, or a spoon tapping against a coffee mug can be used to great effect, depending on the overall tone of your song. Cars backfiring can be used to punctuate a point if you are trying to use found sounds from urban environments, also look for things like the sounds of a swingset, the open and shut off the busses doors, or the chime of the subway station. By now you have probably realized a common theme throughout the book; your musical ability is only limited by your willingness to experiment and the environment you are recording in.

Melodies

The most common type of samples for artists to seek out, are samples that will fill out the melody of their new project. Whether the melody comes from a local artist or a session musician, or even yourself recording and playing the instrument. The key factors to consider when recording these samples are environment and recording equipment. The better you can isolate the sound you want to include in the track from unnecessary frequencies without applying processing FX the better, as this will allow you to be able to apply more processing later when you are editing your sample.

Sometimes you will hear a melody from an old song, or a royalty-free song and you will be able to slice the track into isolated notes that you want to treat in your project. The highest quality audio files you can acquire are necessary for this approach as older recordings can have quite a bit of incidental noise in the recording. This can add a warm, Lo-Fi tone to your music, but if you can gain access to the stems of the original track this will allow you to isolate and process the songs with the same amount of versatility as those who originally mixed the track. The easiest way to obtain the stems of a given song is by entering into remix competitions. This can give you access to more modern samples as quite often established artists will host remix competitions to foster press and momentum for their music.

CHAPTER 7

GETTING STARTED

———————◆○◆———————

The hardest part of a new project is understanding how the flow of your work will achieve the end goals of your project. Before you start to make anything, you need to know what it is that you are trying to make. Is your project just a collection of your latest music, or an anthology informed by themes and movements that span the entirety of your EP? Once you've nailed down your first steps and have found a way to jumpstart your inspiration, you'll be off to the races, but if there are any issues with the rest of the project be sure to read Chapters 8: Problems Progressing, and 9 Finishing your Project. However, taking things one step at a time is extremely important for getting over the hurdle of starting your new project.

Taking the First Steps

Step one of a new recording project is knowing what you want to achieve at the end of your production. You need to assess what you are willing to put into the project in terms of your resources and equipment. Starting a project in the music industry goes beyond simply writing lyrics and notations on a page and slapping a microphone in front of them, although those practices are quite often employed with a bit more tact and care at some point in the early stages of any project.

Project Goals

From a business standpoint, what will this project do to further your portfolio or that of your group? This is extremely important to have established before your creative process can progress past its infancy. Is this your debut Album, a yearly EP, a collection of previously released popular songs? All of these questions bring you closer to what the end goals of your project will be.

For professional musicians, undoubtedly, one of your driving goals is to support yourself at least on a part-time basis but to develop a successful project, you need to have goals beyond

MUSIC PRODUCTION 2022+ EDITION

the basics. What do you need to grow artistically and how can you make this palatable for your listeners? Answering these questions, even in the vaguest sense, will give you a foundation on which to build your project.

Who are you hoping to reach with your message? Music is a personal thing for many listeners and part of the trick to gaining popularity in the music industry is creating a project that people can understand, and that you can convey to as many people as possible while retaining your original message. Some musicians find this a struggle, as any compromise to their original message is seen as a threat to their validity as an artist but being able to explain your point of view in a way that even people who disagree with you can understand is valuable and you will find that you end up swaying minds, and with that, gaining fans.

Resources and Equipment

How much start-up capital do you have to sink into any new resources or instruments that you might need to purchase? This can greatly impact the scope of your project if you are not careful. Creativity can take you a long way, but if you break a mic, can you afford to replace or repair it? Can you hire a session musician if you want to use an instrument you aren't skilled with, in your recording?

How much of an opportunity for a realistic return can you predict on the investment you are prepared to spend? Not every project needs to make money from album sales and downloads alone. For many, they see the majority of their income from the sales of merchandise and tickets for live events.

In a post-Covid world, it's unclear what this might look like, however, as both your ability to perform in a live setting and the willingness of your fans to risk exposure to come to listen to your live performances can be difficult to predict or guarantee. Artists have even begun to explore alternate mediums to release their music, even before a worldwide pandemic struck, such as Marshmello, a renowned EDM producer who performed a live concert in front of millions of viewers in-game. The virtual space allows for a whole new variety of performance art that includes animators and digital art directors. There is a song that was released by The Buggles in 1997 where the chorus repeats the song's titular claim that 'Video killed the radio star.' The song is an anthem-style track that explains the cultural shift in entertainment from radio to television. This caused the advent of music videos and television stations like MTV, and Much Music was originally created to give music videos a platform in the industry. Just like then, the digital space is allowing an all-new and more interactive listener experience than ever, even amid a global pandemic.

Grasping Inspiration

Now that you have the logistical aspects of your project outlined you can set yourself to the task of creating beautiful music for your fans, straight from your heart. You can ensure that you develop your most authentic music by determining a concept for the project as a whole, and how to put that into action.

Project Concept

Usually, a project any given artist releases represents the culmination of an artist's thoughts and experiences within a given emotional range. Kanye West made one of the most iconic breakup albums of all time when he released 808's and Heartbreak in 2004. The album was incredibly clear and direct in terms of the message and tone that West was putting out. If you can harness the essence of your project you can expand on that. Take things one step at a time, one track at a time. If you have a visual memory, it might be a good idea to print out some notes and tape them above your workspace or get a corkboard and make a storyboard for your project so that you at least know what kind of music you need to create for your project.

Remember that every song, EP, album, or series is an opportunity to write and expand on your story. Planning this out and determining a clear vision will help you plan the flow of your work. Which songs are more upbeat? Which songs are sad? Do you need to bring the energy back up after a few darker tracks? It's not a bad idea to select a few possible project layouts and have the music written for any occasion. Sometimes you can't know the final form of the project until you've recorded a few songs and have some momentum built up.

Finally, the last thing you need to do in the early stages of a track is to lay down MIDI tracks to help give you a concept of the project before you step into the recording booth so you can make the most of your studio time.

The Only Way to Start is to Start

Creativity can be incredibly fragile for some artists. Even

outside of the musical discipline, painters, writers, and graffiti artists can all experience the same difficulty finding inspiration for their next project. No matter the discipline, when it's time to start creating, but the ideas refuse to come to you it can be paralyzing and can even send you spiraling into a creativity vortex if you aren't careful. Many professionals in these careers find that just starting to paint or write, whether they be stories, poems, ballads, or sheet music, even if you don't love what you are coming up with, eventually you will strike a vein of gold. Once you do, you just have to follow that golden idea to its source, and you will find your inspiration there waiting for you. You can waste just as much time writing something that lacks inspiration, and maybe stumbling onto that 'gold' as you can lamenting the fact that your creative motivations can't be found. Creativity is a journey, and sometimes you have to chase it to grasp it. The difference is that one of these paths will work through your half-formed ideas and redirect your creative energy around your creative blockage. This can cause you to have a sort of 'Eureka' moment where you end up warming up your brain, (just like any other muscle) before it gets up to speed and can produce the best art possible.

Just like with every lesson this book has to offer so far, your best bet is to devote yourself to practicing if your passions truly motivate you to explore this as a career. The more you practice your instrument, the better your form becomes in playing it, and the easier getting started will become. Even when you think you've found all the note progressions you like, keep experimenting until you find something new, try old ones that maybe you didn't see potential in before but in a new context, they may be the perfect element to ride that lightning into the bottle.

CHAPTER 8

PROBLEMS PROGRESSING

———◆O◆———

Sometimes you find a great idea but after one or two stanzas you find yourself fading and grasping at creative straws. Before you know it, your creative wheels are spinning and for artists who rely on their creative abilities for a living, this can be a serious issue. How can you get back on your creative train? We will be discussing coping mechanisms that will help you with finding your way back to creative bliss and overcome your musician's block.

Musician's Block

Quite often the inability to finish your creative thought or effectively transition it from one to the next is the most daunting prospect for creatives hoping to use their passion to pay the bills. For those who hope to do this one day, or are already doing so, you will need to make sure that you develop several coping mechanisms purely for the sake of shaking off the oppressive influence of Musicians' Block. Depending on your creative process this is something that can be uniquely diverse and personal, therefore, the suggestions that follow may need to be tweaked to give you the best results. In truth, they may serve as little more than inspiration for your unique tips and tricks. Either way, you will find whatever works for you to overcome the greatest challenge to face creative professionals no matter their experience level.

Creative Reserves

Those who are involved in multiple creative pursuits, or those who have been creatively focused for a long time, may have a back catalog of original artwork and inspired ideas that were never fleshed out fully, or never found the proper project to be released. Using these creative reserves will allow you to breathe new life into a forgotten project. Sometimes you need to lay the groundwork of an idea and let it marinate for some time in the recesses of your mind before you are ready to crack that nut and bring your artistic skills to bear.

Sometimes you've already written something that works

perfectly for the project you have designed and all you have to do is rework it. Other times you may have created something in another medium that you want to approach artistically in your music, this can be a great opportunity to lock down cover or album art as well. When you look at your past creativity as a wellspring of ideas you will find you can rejuvenate projects you long gave up on due to a lack of time, money, or writer's block.

The important thing about this technique is that you have to continue to work on your back catalog so that you can renew your reserves, otherwise there will come a day when your reserves run dry! Of course, for many artists, creating is second nature, and ideas strike at wild times. Carry a notepad or record your ideas on your phone so that you can review and execute your brightest notions. If you don't have a back catalog yet though take heart! All you have to do is find the time in your schedule for you to develop these ideas. At first, scheduled creativity may be difficult to force, but over time you will find ways of breaking down those barriers and tapping into your right brain at a moment's notice.

Environment and headspace can be key parts of your creative process so find ways to trigger those feelings and place yourself in the proper environment creatively. You'll find your scheduled creativity sessions much more fruitful, and never underestimate the value of going back and looking over your work from the previous creative session. You will be able to edit the content you produced and tap into the same workflow you managed to get into that session. You will find this allows you to create a bigger and bigger portfolio and the quality of the work you produce will be much higher. There is no shame in revisiting a previous topic you have already covered if you feel like there is more for you to say, or you can say it again in a more coherent or valuable way.

The Distraction Method

Sometimes you are so lost in a creative spiral that you start to produce content that you know is beneath you, or that you fail to put your full effort behind. This can be disheartening and make you feel like you can be wasting creative ideas, or make you feel burnt out. To avoid this, try to have a commitment that doesn't involve music. Many artists will find this role filled by a part-time job, but if you aim to play music professionally you will have to ensure that, firstly, the job is not so taxing that you can't work on your art for a few hours each night. This is difficult to adjust to at first, but the music needs to be one of your top priorities if you hope to make a living. The truth is that there are many talented musicians out there who are capable of playing the same type of music as well or better than you. The difference is between who has made the necessary changes in their lifestyle to make their dreams come true at the end of the day. If you want to play music professionally, you need to work on your craft until you have improved yourself, then you can start to work again. There is no limit to the value that experience will lend you when you are doing something as creative as making music, so pack yourself full of it.

There is a saying that goes, "if you want something done, give it to a busy person." Essentially this means that when someone has a lot to do, they have a diversity of tasks to complete regularly, and this forces them to always be in a productive and working state of mind. This state of mind coupled with the right diversity of responsibilities and creative time can allow for a truly magical synergy of learning and growth. This is another implementation of the distraction method and quite often has the byproduct of forcing you to schedule your time out more, even if you have a full day open, you can dedicate the first two hours to one track, take a small productivity break for about 15 minutes before you continue with the previous track if the inspiration strikes you.

Sometimes you can't get your mind off of that lasagna you made from scratch for your lunches or the show that left you on a cliffhanger last night. Sometimes the best solution to rid yourself of intrusive thoughts is to satiate them, and then get yourself a glass of water, or a cup of coffee and set yourself back to it. This should be exercised carefully however as sometimes this fosters a mood of non-productivity. If you realize that this causes you to become lethargic or distracted, then you should re-evaluate what methods you would like to employ to alleviate your creative fatigue. In small doses, this can result in the optimal balance between work, and recreational time.

Renewing Your Creative Battery

Sometimes you will be in the middle of a musical movement that could make the stars halt their trek across the skies in humbled reverence when suddenly your well of creativity dries up. No matter how hard you try, you cannot seem to produce anything of quality. Creativity always needs inspiration, and you can only draw so much inspiration from your own work. To ensure that you can properly function as a working artist, you need to find a way to recharge your creative battery. This can be done in many ways.

One obvious way to renew your creative battery is to find a way to refresh yourself mentally, physically, or spiritually. Do not underestimate the power of hydration when it comes to the optimal functioning of your mental faculties and your overall mood and wellbeing. Taking a shower will hydrate you and give you a feeling of refreshment. A common phrase can sometimes be heard after someone emerges from a long, satisfying shower; 'Ahhh I feel like a whole new person!' We have a subconscious association between washing ourselves and refreshing our daily cycle. Many people have a habit of showering before work and doing this can do wonders for a fatigued creative mind. On the topic of hydration most importantly, no matter what your artistic process is, make sure that you have an ice-cold glass of water within reach to truly nourish you and flood your body with energy.

Leaving the house or office for a short walk will do wonders for your appreciation of the world around you, and in order to create media, you need to feed your creativity with other media. This means that whether you choose to imbibe media that is new to you or something more familiar and comforting, taking a short break to practice your hobbies or catch up on your favorite shows or artists can be a really rewarding way to give your brain the positivity it needs in order to function at its highest level, and have you feel refreshed and ready to complete your projects to the utmost of your potential.

CHAPTER 9

FINISHING YOUR PROJECT

———◄●O●►———

By now, you have your sounds recorded, you've processed the majority of your sounds to give off the general feeling you want to elicit from your listeners, and you're ready to wrap up your song or project and take it to the next level. Still ahead of you is the mixing process and the mastering process, but there are some final tips for looping and also how to get your music noticed by listeners.

Looping and Production Tips

Looping

One of the most powerful tools in the modern music industry is the looping tool. Some DAWs like FL Studios even have

TOMMY SWINDALI

specialized macros that help with looping functions. Essentially, looping is where you select a section of recorded audio, and you copy and paste that sound to another part of the song. In a live performance, looping can be done through an interface or set of foot pedals to select the looped audio, and then it allows the artist to layer another sound on top of that loop, and so on until the soundscape has reached a point you are happy with.

In the studio, looping can be used to great effect in a number of situations. Artists can experiment and create new musical ideas which they might want to build off of. Musicians could, for example, take one part of a really good piece of recorded audio that has a problem area, but was otherwise the best take, replacing it with a part of the recording where the musician performed the same sequence of notes but better. Looping can be a versatile tool that will save you from many headaches, especially in the Mixing process. While looping is powerful, with great power comes... you get it. Anyways, be careful not to overdo it with looping either. Repeating a single tone over and over again can start to sound robotic and less musical. It may take time and practice to find what the best application for looping is in your own music, but the possibilities it can create with the addition of other processing methods like EQs, and Reverb can be incredibly enticing for listeners if executed properly.

Looping is a tool to keep in mind as you read through Chapter 10: Mixdown, where you will learn about arranging your song or project.

The Logistics of Releasing Your Project

Now that the majority of the creative work has been finished it's time to think about other aspects of your release. There is still plenty of work to be done and a lot of it may end up being the most challenging part of your job as a recording artist. You need to get noticed. At least enough for your fans to know you are working on projects or about to release music or live show dates. Eventually, you will be ready to send your finished music out to a variety of industry professionals. The logistics of this will be outlined in detail in Chapter 12: Getting Signed.

Have you been advertising on social media? Have you dropped any teaser tracks to build interest in your project, even a short clip from a studio session posted to the group social media? These small things can be an impactful way for fans to feel closer to the band and more engaged with your music. Is your group in good standing with local businesses that will allow you to promote your releases and shows? These community ties can make all the difference in who sees your advertisements, and who ends up as a listener and fan of yours.

You need to find a way to engage with your fans if you want them to continue to be invested in your music. Many listeners want to feel connected to the artists in some way so finding your own special way to let your fans know you care about them can go a long way. New listeners are more likely to try to find something in your music to identify with if you can create a sense of community, people with like minds will come together and that fanbase will allow you to develop your art in your most authentic way.

This is a good point in the creation process to start working on your cover art, and liner notes for when you release your music. If you are artistically inclined in the visual sense, this can be a great opportunity for you to flex that muscle and cut some costs at the same time. The cost of professional album art can be pricey and, in order to compensate artists for their time and effort working on your project. You can also use photography as album artwork, this is usually more cost-effective than a digitally designed piece of artwork and you can get multiple shots to choose from. Sometimes the artwork can be as simple as a picture of the artist from their past if that is an aspect, they think influenced the project. Make sure your image is of the highest quality possible as this picture might eventually be blown up to create merchandise like t-shirts and posters which will help increase your revenue.

The creation process is not a straight line and sometimes you can be bouncing between one name or another for a few or maybe even most of your tracks. Now is the time to nail those down. Sometimes taking a memorable line from the song or the chorus can be a good way to name your song if you are having trouble. Other times you can name the song based on your inspiration for the music or even how it makes you feel. Quite often your song titles are one of the easiest things you can do to give your project a cohesive theme for your listeners to imbibe, so take your time and get creative, but use your project as an opportunity to make sure you are conveying the message you want to. Once this is done, naming your project as a whole can become easier if you haven't already thought of something.

Now that you are getting all your ducks in a row it's important to give credit where credit is due right? that means accurately naming your collaborators and the people who helped bring your vision to life. This is also an opportunity to dedicate your project to someone who inspired you to keep creating or even inspired the project in a more direct way. Some artists like to make the final track in their albums a 'goodbye' type track where they thank all the people who came together to make their project a reality; from engineers and inspirations to the friends and even band members who help you let off steam and raise you high when you fall low. These people are an important part of bringing your vision to life and making sure they are appropriately given the credit they deserve is one of the easiest and most impactful ways to thank those who have helped you achieve your goals in one way or another.

Throughout this book, you've read the term 'your project' quite a lot, and you haven't read a whole lot about what kind of project this might be. This is because your project could be a single track you plan to release, a small EP, or even a full-blown album. The difference between a single and the other two types of release is pretty self-explanatory, but EP's and Albums have become more and more interchangeable in the modern recording industry.

There are also a lot of legal responsibilities that accompany releasing your project. Even more so if your music includes samples that you didn't create. Legally you need permission for any samples of someone else's you include in your music. This can be avoided for artists who record their own samples or find royalty-free samples. Remember that you can also freely sample any music 50-75 years after the musician's death depending on the countries you are releasing your music in.

Lastly, one thing to keep in mind is that timing is incredibly important for music releases in the recording industry. For the last seven years, music has been traditionally released on Fridays. While there are two good reasons to do this, the one that originally prompted this was an effort to cut down on piracy. Before then a release from an international artist would be staggered, and impatient listeners in other countries were able to find access to illegal recordings uploaded by music pirates in a country with an earlier release. Countries like Germany and Australia were able to notice, due to the fact that their release date was the latest in the world, that piracy rates were a huge problem. In 2015 the International Federation of the Phonographic Industry (IFPI) which governs almost all music producers in the world set the industry standard across the world for Friday releases. This cut down on piracy due to none of the listeners being able to jump the gun and listen to the album early.

The second good reason for releasing your music on Friday is that's the day people tend to get paid, and they are more likely to be willing to spend money on their favorite artists' new merch, physical and digital copies, and even vinyls. Lining up your musical release with the time of the week when your fans will have the highest spending potential just makes sense.

CHAPTER 10

MIXDOWN

T his is the moment you've been working towards. You have all of your audio files ready to be mixed with only the necessary processing done to it so far that would be integral to the sound of the audio file. You've taken time out to get your logistics sorted out and it's time to enter the mixdown. If you are recording on a physical recording console you begin this process by running the playback outputs of your recording software into the console's line inputs. This will allow you to use the console as a mixing board with all of the onboard processing power it can offer. For many new artists, however, they will just be mixing their music 'in the box,' as they call it, meaning using just a computer and the software. There is absolutely nothing wrong with this method, for many artists outboard processing is too expensive to obtain in the early stages, but once you've got your production setup off the ground, they can be a great addition to your mixdown setup.

In this chapter, you will learn about tone in your projects and the emotional journey you want to take your listeners on. You will also learn about various processing effects and how you might be able to use them in your project.

Tone and Song Arrangement

The tone was briefly defined back in Chapter 1: Song Information. Now might be a good time to go back and review that definition. Once you have done that, think to yourself, what kind of tone you want your project to give off. Both as individual tracks, and as a larger project if you are releasing an album or EP. This gives you the ability to layer your messaging throughout your project. Sometimes this can change the way you arrange songs throughout the project. The song you wrote with the intro track in mind may end up being the outro, or the mid-track that revitalizes the listeners after a more emotionally straining set of songs. It's important to try to take your listeners on a journey rather than a series of tracks giving off the same tones. Use contrast to your advantage and create highs and lows in your project. This will make you a better artist and will also make your music and you as an artist more memorable and relatable.

The mixdown process is the time for you to make all of these decisions. The processing effects discussed later in this chapter will lend themselves to making your tonal design decisions come to bear. For now, focus on the arrangement of your songs. If lyrics are involved, try switching the verses around. The mixdown process is a great time to perform these experiments. The digital age of recording has made this excessively easy, and you can try moving musical movement around within the song. Maybe that one sample with the trumpets should come right before the drop, or maybe they would sound even better as a way to transition out of the drop into your next musical movement. Song arrangement is all about experimentation, and you are only limited by your creativity. If you want to try new ideas, listen to artists you love or admire and look at what they do, try to find your own version of the song arrangement and stick to it. A unique arrangement can do wonders for making your track stand out from others in the project but be careful not to overdo it.

Another important decision when you are arranging your tracks is; to loop or not to loop? Sometimes your musicians will make nearly imperceptible mistakes, but because of your keen ear and knowledge of what the instrument should sound like at that moment, you may consider looping over the mistake from another take or even from an earlier point in the take you are editing. Quite often this is the right move, but there should also be an appreciation for a musician's talent and the small variations from one playthrough to another can also add to the authenticity of your track. If you don't allow any of your natural mistakes to come through in your recorded music two main things will occur. Firstly, the music may sound robotic and almost too perfect if every beat of the drum is 100 percent in time with no variation whatsoever. Secondly, if you go to all the effort of erasing your natural mistakes and quirks, you are giving your listeners an unrealistic expectation for you to live up to a live performance.

Sometimes the small inconsistencies in your performance are what make the greatest impact on your listeners and before long that 'mistake' may be an integral part of the song that your fans would never allow you to leave out. No one can tell you which of these two options is the right one except for you. Trust your artistic vision to withstand a few minor imperfections, otherwise, the music industry may be a difficult pill to swallow in the long run and you will end up burning yourself out or worse; boring your fans. Always try to get a second opinion on your mixdown. After you have been working on a piece for hours on end you can lose your attention to detail and productivity and may not be able to see it until others point it out. It would be much better to happen in the studio than on release day, so bring your project to people whose musical opinions you trust and listen to their criticisms. Keep in mind that they don't have the same emotional attachment to the material and their failure to see your artistic vision is usually not the fault of the listener, but maybe the track is coming in too hot or taking too long to get to the point. Maybe that one mistake you allowed to get through your process isn't as iconic as you were hoping it would seem to other listeners.

Processing, Compression, and EQ

Now that you have your song arrangement lined up it's time to add any processing affects you want to make the individual tracks sound and feel like a cohesive musical movement. There are a number of processing effects, many of which are available in both analog and digital equivalents that you can apply to your music to give it a unique sound!

Compression and EQ

Equalizers are really a form of compression. The difference is that while a compressor plugin will compress the entire frequency range; an equalizer can be applied to a very specific frequency range and usually they come equipped with variables that you can apply. Some Equalizers are even able to compress multiple points along the frequency spectrum individually, these are called multiband compressors. Compression should be used sparingly as it is often a part of the mastering process, so if you intend to master your project you may want to be careful with using too much compression during the mixdown phase.

There is also another form of compression referred to as Hi and Low Filters. These are highly effective compression devices that will remove all sounds above or below a specified frequency. These can be great for removing room noise from drum recordings or anything that needs to be isolated in order to be treated in a particular manner. Usually, any microphones on the cymbals should not be filtered if you can help it as a good amount of room noise contributes to a natural feeling that one gets if they were to actually see the song performed live.

Reverb

If you have ever attended a large place of worship like a cathedral, mosque, or large temple you will likely have noticed a naturally reverberative quality to the space inside. For this reason, many accomplished singers even rent out these spaces to perform or record due to the natural beauty that the architecture brings to the soundwaves making up their music. If possible, you should always attempt to apply a natural reverberative quality during the recording phase to any sounds you think might benefit from it due to its naturally ethereal quality. That said, there is nothing wrong with using a plugin to apply the effect during the mixing phase. Just be aware that reverb should be used in precise amounts, too much can be overwhelming for your listeners.

Grouping

Grouping is a relatively simple production technique, but it can have some profound effects on your mixing process. By applying groups to your tracks, you can assign a channel to control all of your drum sounds once you have them mixed and moving the fader that controls the group will raise or lower gain equally across all the grouped channels. This can make a huge difference for pretty much any producer, but especially EDM and Hip-Hop producers will find that when songs get up to over 100 channels, you will need one or two groups to manage the sheer number of recorded sounds you are controlling.

Pitch Shifting

Sometimes after you have recorded a sound you realize that it would have fit better into the song if it was just an octave higher or lower in pitch. Using this tool, you can correct that or even use this tool to alter specific parts of a recording rather than the recording as a whole. If there are any major changes in pitch to be done you may want to record the sound again, but sometimes this isn't possible, or perhaps you like the slightly overproduced tone this will create.

Ultimately, mixing is a subjective art form, and you should experiment with it as much as possible. If you continue to practice mixing your music you will discover all sorts of creative ideas, you didn't even know you had locked in your mind! These pages can merely serve as your guide in this endeavor, but there is no substitute for repetition and practice if you would like to reach your full potential as a mixing engineer.

CHAPTER 11

MASTERING

———————◆◇◆———————

Mastering is the practice of combining multiple tracks in series to create an overall tone and artistic vision for the listeners to tap into and follow along with. This process involves creating transitions between different tracks and placing specific gaps between songs. In this chapter, you will learn not only why musicians master their music, but whether or not you should master your musical project. You will also learn some of the basic techniques and requirements for mastering a project in the modern music industry.

Why do Musicians Master Their Music?

Typically, musicians master their music because each track is recorded and mixed at different times. This can make differences in sound levels, and processing choices from one track to another. Even just spacing out tracks so that they don't run into each other or adding a last-minute interlude to buffer between one song and another. If mixing is putting a coat of paint on a new car, mastering is like the polish you put on the car to make it shine and repel rain droplets.

Compression

Musicians employ compression in the mastering process only when they are trying to tie multiple tracks together with varying levels of gain. When you apply compression to an album you reduce the sonic range throughout the entire piece. This can give your music a feeling of togetherness or oneness but take care; don't overuse compression. If you use too much compression your songs will become muddled and sounds that were supposed to be cohesive with other instruments are now fighting for the reduced bandwidth over-compression can cause in the mastering process.

Compression has become one of the main standards of mastering. Nearly all mastering engineers will apply compression to a project no matter what, but this can be a mistake in some cases, if compression has already been used during the mixing phase or if the track will be released as a single. This gives you the freedom to allow a song to explore its full range of tonality. Many artists will release multiple versions of their songs as both a single and as a larger project. The songs will be nearly identical to most listeners, but there will be slight changes in the mixing and if there is compression added in the mastering phase this will change the sonic range of the song to be more uniform throughout the project.

Interludes

Sometimes your music can take people on a rollercoaster of emotions from one song to another. Even with proper transitioning and compression, this gap can sometimes be too large to bridge in a project, but you are unwilling to change the order of the tracks for artistic reasons. This can be a good moment to use an interlude. This was a technique first employed in Hip-Hop and Rap music as a way to divide albums into different moods. If one song is too emotionally intense to naturally be followed up by that more up-beat party anthem you intended to use as a vessel to bring the mood up, you can add a small break in the music lasting anywhere from a few seconds to a minute for more impactful or humorous interludes.

Quite often interludes are a break from music. Originally it was a popular choice to use recorded phone conversations or voicemails, but since then people have started using recited scripture, or speeches from a politician the artist admires or admonishes. Lately, a trend has even developed where interludes are purely instrumental, and the vocals don't play a part at all. This can be especially useful for people looking to give their listeners a break from a more intense lyrical barrage in one song and should usually be followed up by a sharp shift in mood afterward to give listeners a sense of contrast. This can be a valuable tool in a process that is mostly geared towards making multiple musical works into a single series.

Crossfading and Transitions

Transitions between your tracks can be extremely important for the tone you are trying to evoke from your listeners while mastering a project. Some projects allow for a half-beat of total silence between each track to allow listeners to mark the differences between the end of one track and the beginning of another. Other projects have been designed to be released as a complete unit and the tail end of one song might line up perfectly with the introduction of the next track. This is an important artistic decision to be made long before the time of recording your project. If you already have all of your mixed tracks and would like to add these blended transitions then it is likely too late, and your best bet of achieving this effect is with short interludes to bridge one song to another, but there is nothing wrong with leaving space for your listeners to think between each song.

Regardless of whether you are transitioning from one song to another seamlessly, with transitions or with a definitive pause, crossfading will come into play. This is a very important thing for artists to remember. This small task can be easy to overlook especially if you are transitioning with a blended transition or with an interlude, but as listeners of music you expect that transition between tracks, otherwise, they sound too much like separate entities and not consecutive entries in a cohesive project. If you gradually, and swiftly lower the gain at the end of one track, and then gradually, and swiftly raise the gain again at the beginning of the next piece of audio this will have two effects. Firstly, it will remove the small 'click' or 'pop' you can hear at the very end of a piece of recorded audio. Secondly, it will make your transition more impactful and cohesive with the music on either side of it.

When You Should Master Your Music

Not every piece of music needs mastering. This can be difficult for new people and even more established industry professionals to wrap their heads around. The fact is that mastering a project quite often requires specialized skills and equipment and requires a sensitive ear. This skill takes more practice than most of the other concepts you've learned so far, which is why it's one of the final steps in your lessons. Before you master anything and release it, listen to it, and make notes alongside other music you know has been mastered. Think about how that artist was able to achieve things you maybe weren't able to. Through investigation and experimentation, you will eventually give yourself enough experience to build a solid understanding of the values and challenges that accompany mastering a track.

Beyond this, not every track needs to be mastered. Perhaps all the recordings were done one after another and the mixing followed the same pattern. When this is the case and the tracks are mixed by a skilled engineer with adequate equipment, you may find that your project has a feeling of authenticity and togetherness even without applying large-scale mastering effects. This can do wonders for your bottom line as mastering-quality compressors and processors can be very expensive and hiring an experienced mastering engineer can be even more costly for their hourly rates.

CHAPTER 12

GETTING SIGNED

———————◄●►———————

You just finished recording, mixing, and mastering your artistic project. You have the album artwork finished, and you've written your liner notes. By now if you haven't found someone to buy or distribute your project, you will want to make it your first priority. Organized artists will start this process before the time comes for the project to reach completion.

Sending Music Out

Sending out the music that you've put all of your artistic energy into can be very taxing and anxiety-inducing for artists. Take heart, knowing that this is natural, and an essential part of trying to get your music distributed on a larger scale. The quest for representation is grueling and along the way, you may receive feedback. This is a good outcome and is given from a desire of the label representative to help you develop your music and skills. Even if they are not ready to invest in you yet, persevere, and learn from failures to find your path forward. Each rejection is a learning opportunity, it is up to you to determine the lesson and apply it to your situation. This aspect of the music industry is no different from anything else covered in this book. Repetition is necessary for learning and long-term success.

Labels

Labels are a part of the music industry that represent artists in their quest to distribute their music and message to as many ears as possible! There are many labels out there to consider both large and small. When you are looking for labels to pursue the most important thing is to look for people who would understand and appreciate both your genre of music and your style of play. There are a massive number of labels out there and many different considerations can affect your choice, like where the label is active, the connections they promote having, and the size of the label. All of these factors can make a huge difference in what labels you might want to focus the most of your energy on.

It's important not to message as many labels as possible, but to focus on finding the right fit to ensure you find someone who appreciates and wants to safeguard your music. Otherwise, you may end up getting offers that don't necessarily have your best interests at heart, or you'll get no response at all. This is easily one of the biggest mental challenges that face an artist who is seeking representation. Resist the urge to get the project released quickly, without doing your due diligence with the people who will facilitate that process for you.

Investigate the connections the labels you are courting have. What platforms are that label's artists on? Are those platforms spaces where you believe your music will have the opportunity to succeed? These considerations can make a huge difference from one label to the next.

Addressing Correspondence

Most times when you are reaching out to a record label you won't be trying to slip a demo under an executive's doors or anything like that, and no, commenting your SoundCloud link in Instagram comment sections won't cut it either. There is a procedure and proper way to approach these labels. Knowing the etiquette can be the difference between having your correspondence read, or discarded and even marked as spam, from which there is no coming back.

Your message to a prospective label should include a short bio about you and your group. You don't need to get too wordy but give them an idea of the personality and charisma of the group, and how you would use that to attract listeners. Follow that up with a brief explanation of your demo piece including what stage of production it is in. It's okay to demo an unfinished song as long as the label representative can make the connection between your art and the stage of completion your project has reached, but always send out the most recent version of your demo to give the label the best idea of your capabilities.

You should try not to put too much effort into approaching more than four labels at a time. Doing this allows you to narrow your focus and ensure your correspondence is unique considering the label, the type of artists they represent, and the connections they maintain. If you approach too many labels at one time it is too hard to resist the urge to create a formulaic message structure that label representatives can recognize instantly and could even mean getting your messages marked as spam.

Patience

The most important attribute to practice when you are approaching labels for representation is patience. Showing your ability to be resilient in the face of adversity shows labels you have what it takes to be disciplined within the music industry. Don't forget this is far more business than art for the record label. More than that, record labels receive an amount of correspondence with such sheer quantities that you may just need to try and try again. The representative might not have seen your message because of a busy day, or an accidental click gone unfixed. Regardless, a non-response is not a rejection. Until you receive definitive communication from the label that indicates they have no intentions of representing you, keep trying. Not only does this show spirit and determination, but also shows consistency, which can be a rare commodity in the music industry.

Tips and Tricks

Finding representation for your group can be daunting! To help you persevere through the hardest part of your job there are a few final topics to go over. The role of confidence in the music industry is just the tip of the iceberg. Having more than one Demo to send out can be advantageous as well. Finally, networking is important, and quite often the fun part of trying to break into the music industry. With that, you should have most of the tools in your arsenal that you'll need to begin your foray into the professional music industry.

The Role of Confidence in the Music Industry

Putting your artwork that you've invested your time and your passion into, out in the world for others to criticize is not easy, and hopefully, no one ever told you it would be. It's going to be hard, and probably emotionally difficult at times. This is why it's more important than ever that during this phase of your career you don't forget your value and what you have to offer record labels. Keeping a realistic opinion of your talent helps ensure that labels, first of all, are less likely to try to give you a poor deal that doesn't work in your favor, and if they do, there's more of a chance they will respect you when you confidently tell them, 'No thank you. With the hard work and time that goes into our music, this arrangement won't compensate our group to the level that we require for this to be a worthwhile venture for all parties.' Always be prepared to negotiate on these terms and be firm on your limits.

There is another side to this coin. If you exude confidence to the point where it seems forced or inauthentic, or even if it's just unfounded confidence from the label's point of view. It's important to balance confidence with humility. The two concepts may seem like opposites, but with care, you can achieve an equilibrium between them. People like to feel like they will be able to work with your group, and that you will be open to criticism and direction up to a certain point, so showing some humility can go a long way towards showing the label representatives your maturity. If you can manage to balance your pride and your humility when you speak with labels, you will find people treat you with the respect your music commands. The old adage 'don't judge a book by its cover,' is a heartwarming and wise sentiment, but the reality of the music industry is that if you can't present a marketable face to the labels, they won't be able to sign you, even if your music is good! To paraphrase Kendrick Lamar, 'Be Humble, Sit Down.'

How Many Demos is Too Many?

When you send your Demos out to labels you may have more than one prospective piece of music to send in. Your urge may be to send your whole album and see what they think, however, this can be overwhelming for busy label representatives who barely have two minutes to listen to a demo before deciding if the group is worth looking into or not.

When you are looking for what track to use as a demo, try to find the one that first of all represents the best of what each of the members of your group has to offer, and if possible, something that allows every musician to shine. If you have multiple mixes of the same song, it may be beneficial to send a second mix that is clearly labeled as the same track at a different point of production. Also, ensure that this mix is sonically independent enough from the other. If all you've added is a little more reverb on the vocals, they probably don't need to see that artistic journey. This can help give the labels an idea of where you came from and where you are now in your recording process and musical talent.

Networking in the Music Industry

Networking is one of the most natural things to happen at live music events. Music naturally brings people together and those who love to create it usually love to share it too. This has become difficult over recent years with the Covid Pandemic, which came to North America in March 2019. Musicians who used to be able to network with fans and other artists, not to mention label representatives, have found the loss of intimate interaction with their fanbase and ability to grow their fanbase with live venues and people playing new music at parties and other gatherings to be a devastating blow to their growth. Given these new challenges, there are a few tips both for those who can safely perform live music and interact with their fans.

Live Shows

If you can hold live shows and in-person meetings then you need to be aware of any Covid regulations and guidelines that affect the venue you'll be performing at, and if you need to arrange accommodation you need to ensure the place of accommodation follows the same or stricter guidelines as the venue. Make sure the venue will have masks, and hand sanitizer, also that the bathrooms remain well-stocked and maintained throughout the show.

Aside from Covid precautions, there are plenty of opportunities to learn and connect at live venues. Whether the show is one you are performing at, or you are an audience member at another group's show, both are great networking opportunities. If you encounter other musicians at a venue, feel free to exchange information. If you have permission from the performing group and the venue, you can even promote your shows on later dates. Musicians don't need to compete for consumers as other professions do. People who like one brand of pop music will probably enjoy another artist who plays a similar style of music within their genre too. If groups become close enough, they might even collaborate on each other's music and perform at each other's shows. This exposes the fanbase of one band to the talents of another group. As an emerging artist, your best hope to gain a following and exposure is to find a way to work on a project with another group as well-known as you or more well known.

Remember that like with approaching labels, promoting your shows at venues requires humility. Not everyone will be interested, and you need to be cognizant that if this isn't your show, you may not be welcome to promote yourself. While the music industry is collaborative, it's always best to safeguard your relationships with your fellow musicians and the people who enjoy their music.

Networking in the Age of Covid

In the last three years, the ability of musicians to network with their fans and other creative types has been decimated. Any artist looking to build a fanbase in these times needs to be realistic about the challenges that they face. Do not lose hope though, there are still ways to get your music and your group out into the world. There are online music-sharing platforms that can be a great opportunity to get out there. Soundcloud is just one of those sites, but YouTube is another site with very high traffic. Keep in mind you will likely need a visual component to post to YouTube, even if it's just cover art. Twitch is a live streaming service with a section specifically for musicians to stream their music and their creative process with their fans and other creative types. In the age of Covid, opportunities like this are the closest musicians can get to the interaction they were able to achieve with their fans at a live performance. Lastly, in the age of Covid, more people are staying inside and consuming digital media than ever before. One of the best ways to boost your awareness among fans and other creative people is by trying to get your music included in the media people to consume daily. This means sending your music to podcasts, YouTubers, video game developers. In the age of covid, these are the easiest to reach professionals with the widest reach to your fanbases. Even without Covid, this would be a good thing to do to boost awareness of your music, but now it has become a necessity.

CHAPTER 13

FREQUENTLY ASKED QUESTIONS

———————◄O►———————

What is a Music Producer?

A Music Producer is a professional who takes recorded pieces of audio and arranges them to achieve the best sonic result possible. The portfolio of a producer can also include engineering the song, if need be, by applying processing effects and making artistic decisions about the track in the mixing phase. Producers are responsible for the success of the project, and sometimes they may even be required to send music out to labels for the artist! Although it's not uncommon for emerging artists to play the role of musician, audio engineer, and producer all at once. Doing three jobs yourself saves on a lot of expenses!

Is my Musical Group a Business?

The short answer, kind of! However, there are a lot of things you need to decide and do before you can call your group a bonafide business! First, you need to decide the legal structure of your group. Meeting with a tax specialist can be a great idea at this stage they will tell you what legal structure makes the most sense for you.

You'll also need to file for a business license from your county clerk's office. In some countries, you may also need to file for a tax ID for the new business that is separate from yours. This can help protect people involved in the event of financial insolvency.

Open an account specifically for the business. No personal expenses or contributions should be made, and the business account should be strictly controlled and only accessed for specific, group-related costs, like paying for studio time or accommodations while traveling.

Start tracking the expenses and the revenue from your musical ventures, the more documentation you have, the more accurate your tax claim will be! This also allows for the possibility of a company card. These small changes can make a big difference in how people will think about your band. Being prepared makes you look successful and looking successful quite often makes you successful.

Tax Time is Coming, Can We Write Anything Off?

You should keep track of all expenses made in the name of the group. To write off an expense, it needs to meet certain qualifications. Your claims must all be ordinary business expenses that were necessary to run the business. This can mean phone expenses, graphic design charges, office supplies, advertising costs, travel costs, and meals. Even your rent can be deducted if you do enough of your work at home. If you ever need to hire legal professionals for your business these can be written off too, even wages can be written off if you keep any employees on retainer.

There is of course a catch to writing off your business expenses. If you are not turning a profit after five years your business will be classified as a hobby, and you will lose all of the business eligible deductions that make your business so viable. You need to prove that you've run a profit two out of five years to maintain your business classification. That said, if you are trying to classify your musical group as a business you want it to be profitable, otherwise, you won't be able to support yourself while you pursue your passions.

CONCLUSION

Well done!

You've completed reading Music Production for Beginners 2022 Edition! Throughout this book, you will have gleaned all the information you require from these pages to be successful in your musical pursuits. Now that you have this knowledge it's time for you to put this information into practice. There are still many obstacles ahead of you but armed with the knowledge in this book you'll have the extra boost you'll need to overcome them! This book will always be here if you need to reference it again, there is a lot of information in here! Even now that you have finished this book you should continue practicing the techniques you have learned every day and always try to find the next growth path. Just because the book is finished, doesn't mean that practice isn't one of the most important things to do if you want to improve your craft.

Don't forget that this book is not meant to be the only tool in your toolbelt! It will help you navigate the YouTube videos and other tutorials that may have mystified you before now, but you should always be looking for new sources to learn and grow from! You have all the passion you need to create the music you want; you just need to learn how to tap into that passion and express it beautifully through your art.

If you decided to try this book because you didn't like the sounds of hiring a recording engineer or renting out an expensive recording studio then you might even have your home recording studio or mixing and mastering space by now! This is a great way to cut costs for musicians who want to work in the music industry long-term.

Once you have your own recording space you can even rent it out to try to offset the financial costs of setting up a proper recording space. You could also offer to mix music for other groups for a fee, this is one of the easiest ways to solve monetary issues when you are in this industry because many artists know how to play and even record, but mixing takes skill and practice which other musicians may not have invested in.

For readers without any formal training or knowledge in the music industry, you get a very special congratulations. Your passion must be strong to have brought you down the path of learning from novice musician to mastering engineer. Not everyone has the strength of spirit or desire to make art and share it with the world, especially if they are learning later. There is no wrong time to learn these skills, and new skills can only diversify your marketability and your life experiences.

This book should have served as a roadmap to allow you to find inspiration and knowledge for you to incorporate into your music. Now you can take your artistic vision and turn it into a well-polished, market-ready project for you to break into this vast industry and make your mark on the world of music.

On days when things are getting to be coming at you too fast, come back and read over a few relevant pages of this book and then come and read the conclusion again to give yourself a boost through the other side of those dark days! Remember that there will be ups and downs. You will make bad music on your path to create art but take heart and keep creating! Keep writing! Keep playing! Your musical talents will only fade if

you stop feeding them!

GLOSSARY

Acoustics - The Science of the production, transmission, reception, and effects of sound.

Acoustic Treatment - Using various architectural techniques to modify how soundwaves react in the space. This also affects how the listener perceives the sound.

Background/Room Noise - Unwanted sound naturally produced by the recording environment that you do not want to be included in the recording.

Bar - In a piece of sheet music, a Bar is a vertical line that spans the musical staff before the original measure accent.

Bass - The Lower end of the frequency spectrum falls in the Bass Clef. All octaves lower in frequency than Middle C are on the Bass Clef.

Bass Trap - A device that can help remove frequencies that resonate too strongly in a space used for professional quality recording or viewing/listening. Specifically designed to remove lower frequency resonant tones. Usually placed in corners or against walls opposite the sound source.

Beat - a rhythmic metric used in music and poetry to mark the rhythmic stresses of the musical piece.

Compression - A production technique applied at the time of recording or during the Mixdown phase of the project to reduce dynamic range from a specific tonal point.

Cover Art - an illustration or photograph used to represent the feeling and tone of a musical project. Usually displayed on streaming services, merchandise, and physical copies of the project.

Cymbal - A concave metal plate that is usually made of brass that produces high-frequency clashing sounds when struck either with a drumstick, or another Cymbal. Sometimes multiple Cymbals are included in a drum arrangement.

Digital Audio Workstation (DAW) - A common software tool used by music professionals to record and mix musical sounds. The use of this software has become an industry requirement for anyone who wants to participate in the industry.

Electronic Music - Music that places its focus on manipulating electronically produced signals and arranging them to emit a rhythm and tone forming into a melody, and rhythm.

Foley - Sound effects produced for use in a film. Often replaces or emphasizes the environmental sound effects present in the scene.

Folk Music - The traditional music of a country or region that uses local techniques and instruments to create music with a specific tone. Usually, folk music does not include electronic instruments.

Frequency - refers to the sound created by the number of complete oscillations per second in the form of soundwaves.

Frequency Response Curve (FRC) - is a graph that represents how a device reacts to certain frequencies. With Decibels on the X-axis and frequency on the Y-axis; you can see what frequencies are dominant when they are filtered through this device.

Hi-Hat - A pair of cymbals, one of which is inverted affixed to a metal pole and controlled by a foot pedal that brings one cymbal closer to the other.

Hi/Low Toms - Larger drums of varying sizes create a higher or lower timbre depending on their size. Low toms being largest. The instrument emits a bassy, open tone.

Hip-Hop - Stylised and rhythmic music, sometimes accompanied by rap lyrics. Usually, music from this genre will make use of samples and the sound effects are likely heavily processed, although there is a movement within Hip-Hop of using analog sounds to fill out the melody and balance out the heavy rhythmic presence.

Hertz (Hz) - A unit of measurement for how many sonic oscillations occur per second.

International Federation of the Phonographic Industry (IFPI) - A worldwide organization that represents more than 1,400 companies and associations. Their primary focus is protecting the rights of record producers and expanding the use of recorded music.

Key - Is tones and harmonies that are represented by seven tones in a hierarchical arrangement.

Kick - a part of a drum set that is the largest component out of all the others. Operated with a foot pedal to create a bassy, impactful strike. Usually, this drum marks the rhythm of the other musicians in the group.

Liner Notes - explanatory notes written by the artist about the project, usually including thank-you's to influential people on the project and giving credit to all the people who came together to make your project a reality.

Looping - Replaying a recorded audio sound, musical or not. The loop can be repeated indefinitely, with a short delay, or repeated just a few times. All of these are different examples of the looping technique.

Mastering - Using production techniques to turn multiple tracks into a single cohesive EP or album including transitions between tracks and compressing the project as a whole to help the project sound like one cohesive project rather than multiple individual projects linked together.

Measure - a grouping of a specified number of beats between two bars on a sheet music staff.

MIDI - Musical Instrument Digital Interface is an electronic standard across the music industry used for the quality transmission of digital music.

Mixing - Combining the recorded audio you have selected for a musical project and processing it to create a complete musical entity.

Note - a symbol used in sheet music to simultaneously indicate duration, pitch, and tone based on what shape the note takes and where it rests on the staff.

Octave - a complete series of notes ranging from A to G which make up the units of a modern scale.

Pitch - is a term used to describe the sonic attributes that different frequencies can provide. A sound that feels higher than another is simply in another pitch. This is how you can play two C notes in different octaves and the note is still the same, it is just being played at a different pitch.

Plugins - Can be both physical hardware, or software you can purchase and integrate into your DAW. They are usually used to add or enhance audio recordings. Usually, plugins will feature their own interface independent of your recording software, even if you are using a software plugin.

Rap - rhythmic music usually created by African American people featuring lyrics that usually rhyme and are chanted to music.

Reverb - an electronically produced echo effect used in music to create a more dynamic and emotional soundscape.

Rhythm and Blues - a musical genre that includes elements of blues with African American folk music. The genre features a simple chord structure and a strong beat.

Royalty-Free - Samples that are Royalty-free only require a one-time payment for you to use an unlimited number of times, even in future projects.

Sample - an excerpt from a recorded piece of audio, usually created by another recording artist that can be incorporated into your own music with the owner's permission.

Scales - an arpeggiating series of musical tones that progress in either descending or ascending tones across a specified number of octaves.

Sheet Music - notation and other musical information that has been printed onto large sheets of paper for musicians to refer to when playing or practicing.

Snare - one of the smallest drums in a typical drum setup.

Song Arrangement - taking pre-recorded audio and changing it from its original place in the song to another place that makes a stronger impact.

Soundwaves - pressure waves created by the vibration of one piece of matter interacting with another. Not all soundwaves can be heard by the human ear.

Studio Monitors - Powered speakers that usually require external gain control. Studio Monitors have a more efficient design than commercial speakers with a focus on the sonic treatment of the soundwaves passed through them.

Subwoofer - A specifically designed speaker with only the lowest frequencies in mind since it requires specific hardware to emulate those frequencies.

Synthesizers - a computerized electric apparatus that can be used to produce and control sound to produce musical tones.

Tabs - a visual representation of instrumental notation indicating finger position instead of using typical sheet music notation.

Tempo - the rate of speed a piece of music is played at, sometimes sheet music can provide direction on when to alter the temp with largo, presto, and allegro notations. Can be measured with a metronome.

Tone - a sound of precise pitch and vibration.

Treble - The upper half of the tonal range of the instrument. anything above Middle C is considered to reside in the treble clef.

Tweeter - a small speaker head that is responsible for producing only the highest frequencies, and usually requires specific construction to create.

USB - (Universal Serial Bus) is a standardized hardware interface used to transmit signals to peripheral devices.

XLR - a standardized hardware interface used in professional audio equipment featuring a balanced connection that locks securely into its socket.

MUSIC PRODUCTION SONGWRITING, & AUDIO ENGINEERING, 2022+ EDITION

The Professional Guide for Music Producers, Songwriters & Audio Engineers in Music Studios

INTRODUCTION

April 9, 1860, marks the planting of the seed that would blossom into the music industry; the very first recording of sound. Predating the first phone call and phonograph by sixteen and seventeen years respectively, the very first recording of sound came in the form of an eerie, spine-chilling recording of Au Claire de la Lune on Parisien inventor, Édouard-Léon Scott de Martinville's creation, the phonautograph. The recordings were never intended to be listened to in the same way we do in the modern day. Instead, they were meant to help us understand exactly how we hear. The machine recorded the vibrations of sound, those tracings meant to help us read sound, rather than listen to it. It was not until the phonograph was introduced that listening to those recordings was considered by anyone. Since that point, music production has grown and developed beyond Scott de Martinville's wildest dreams and expectations.

Today, our technology has evolved to be far more accessible. Anyone who can get their hands on some basic equipment can start their journey into music production. With some practical skill development, proper marketing, and some tech, such as microphones, a computer, and some research, anyone can build themselves a studio to begin their musical journey. Today's advancements can be overwhelming to a new producer or musical artist; different software, pedals, soundboards, and so much more have allowed us to create music like never before and it has given us the freedom of creativity that is so untapped, it is a little overwhelming. New genres pop up all over the place, new artists are sampling sounds from decades before, and old trends are finding themselves revamped in all kinds of ways.

Because of this incredible flexibility within the musical tools we have today, it is impossible to tell anyone the tools they need to master to produce their ideal sound. We still see artists who make music via traditional instruments, just like we have music producers who have never touched an instrument in their lives, instead of creating their music using their technology, such as phones and laptops. Music producers and artists are gathering their preferred equipment, developing their methods, and fine-tuning their sounds in ways that define them and set them apart in a world where anyone can create a track on an app from their phone. What truly sets these people apart isn't just their technical skills and their ability to create a musical masterpiece, but it is also the way they sell themselves.

Career Goals in the Music Industry

Exactly where do you see yourself wanting to be in the music industry? Chances are, if you're holding this book, you might hope to see yourself become the next Max Martin or Dr. Dre. Maybe you are hoping to make waves as a self-produced vocalist or band. Perhaps you want to be involved in the production process, but with a special focus, such as one of the following:

- **Arranger**

An arranger examines the whole of the composed piece and gives each element of the track new life. They adjust everything from vocals to tempo to instrumentation to revitalize a track and bring it all together.

- **Composer**

A composer writes and directs a piece of music. Consider artists such as Hans Zimmer and Danny Elfman, who create powerful soundtracks for movies and more.

- **Lyricist**

A lyricist's job is to create engaging hooks and to fill in the story of the song with creative, catchy, and unique lyrics.

- **Mixing Engineer**

A mixing engineer gathers all of the components of the recording, making sure they blend seamlessly, and masters the track into its final product,

- **Music Producer**

A music producer is hands-on in helping the artist create their vision. They may help the artist work on an area of the work the artist is not happy with, or they can help clean up the track in a way that bumps it up to the next level. A music producer may employ a team of people, but generally, they tend to be a jack-of-all-trades in producing the overall product.

- **Orchestrator**

If a composer writes a piece of music, an orchestrator is the one who brings the writing to life in performance.

- **Songwriter**

Being a songwriter can be a multipurpose job. While a lyricist focuses on providing lyrics to the track, a songwriter can be hands-on in both developing and writing the music for the track, as well as the lyrics that will be going over the music.

- **Sound Designer**

A sound designer is the one who will search for the sounds to be used on the track. This could mean pulling samples from other tracks. It could also mean using clips of speech or sounds from popular media. Some sound designers go as far as to create a new sound if there is a copyright on the sound the artist was hoping to use. They also utilize commercial audio libraries to provide unique sounds for the artist's track.

Welcome to the Music Industry

Finding success in the industry in the modern age is an absolute paradox; on one hand, we still reach for the traditional methods of finding success through labels and production companies. On the other hand, we can see multitudes of people creating success through clever and continuing work online, whether it's on YouTube, Tiktok, SoundCloud, or any other social platform. The path to music industry success has continued to develop and splinter off, and it means that anyone willing to put in the work, passion, and time can potentially create a career for themselves.

New artists, full of enthusiasm and determination, can sometimes fall into the trap of thinking that, as long as they are producing what they consider to be a masterpiece, success will fall into their lap. Some producers or executives will be surfing social media, hear the magical hook they have created, and demand that they sign a deal with them immediately. However, that is not how it works. These days, producers aren't hanging out in clubs and SoundCloud pages hoping to find fresh talent and someone that can take from a nobody to the top. Instead, it's crucial that new artists distinguish themselves, build an audience, and then work their way through the pack to make a name for themselves.

Raw talent is not everything. If you are putting time into developing your music, you need to be putting that same amount of time into developing your presence, audience, and reach in the music industry. When we see successful artists in the music industry, we see the party, the energy, the fire in their live performances, and the wildlife they portray on their social media and in their music videos. What we don't see are the hours spent in the studio fine-tuning their tracks, slamming their head into the wall while trying to find the lyrics that represent what they want to say. We do not see the marketing meetings, the time spent awake until four in the morning as they write, finesse, and develop their music. Nor do we see the blisters from repeatedly playing the same chords or the time they need to care for and maintain their voice after days or weeks in front of the microphone. We do not see the hours and hours required to develop the content of their music videos, the planning logistics of tours and concerts. Raw talent will give you something to work with, but that's only the seed that provides you your start; there is a lot more work to be done to get that seed to grow.

With all of this in mind, where does that leave a budding producer? Well, it leads you right here, in the hands of someone with over twenty years of experience, knowledge, and insight. This is the book that teaches more than just how to plug in your microphone and tack on some reverb; this is where you learn to adjust your mindset, develop the drive behind your music, and take your music up a notch (or ten.) No matter where you are starting from, this is where you figure out the next step on the road ahead. Welcome to Music Production. Let's see who you can become.

CHAPTER 1

BASIC ELEMENTS OF MUSIC

———————◄O►———————

If you are looking to make a career for yourself in music, it is a good idea to know the fundamentals of sound and music. This chapter will provide a brief overview of these fundamentals for quick reference.

Beat

The beat is what helps to regulate the pattern of rhythm. Typically, the beat is set by percussion.

Dynamic

Dynamics provide the volume, both in general and in providing emphasis in the music. The dynamic is measured in decibels. You will often see decibels written as dB, dBs (for multiple decibels), or dBFS (decibels relative to full scale) which relates to your gain controls.

Harmony

Harmonies happen when two or more notes are played simultaneously. The harmony is both the support and the texture behind the song's melody.

Melody

The melody is the tune, or a succession of notes, tones, and pitches that create a pleasant listening experience.

Meter

Meter relates to your beat or rhythm. Meter is commonly counted in beats of two or four.

Pitch

Pitch relates to frequency. Where frequency is the measurement of sound waves, the faster the vibration and more active the soundwave, the higher the pitch. The slower the vibration and the larger the vibration source, the lower pitch.

Rhythm

Meter, tempo, and beat come together to form the rhythm. This is the pattern that creates the flow of the song, and it is the foundation of the melody.

Tempo

Tempo indicates the speed of the music and how quickly the components within the song are moving.

Texture

Texture comes from how many layers there are in your song. This can come from the variety of instruments in the song, the chords, or the harmonies and effects used in the song.

Timbre

Timbre describes the quality of the sound. It could be bright, dark, muddy, dull, or clean.

CHAPTER 2

STUDIO BASICS

——————◄O►——————

Back in the day (you know, literally a decade ago) there was a driving desire to get into a large, professional studio when it came time to record the music you have been working day and night to create. Now, we see a boom of "bedroom studios." Artists are collecting their beginner equipment and recording their tracks right there on the bedside table. Of course, this slowly evolves into finding dedicated space to create a home studio and potentially continues its evolution into a professional set-up, either at home or in another location. Bedroom and at-home studios aren't going anywhere soon, so knowing how to arrange your set-up, buy the perfect equipment, and choose the best space is crucial for new music producers and artists.

Choosing the Room

Not all rooms are equal. When choosing the room you want to arrange your studio in, you have to consider a variety of factors.

1. How high are your ceilings? Using a room with low ceilings can mean facing a nightmare when recording. What you want to consider is the reflection of the noise as your mic is picking up sound. Too low of a ceiling can create what is called comb filtering. This happens when the sound is being bounced back to the microphone in a way that it picks it up over and over again.

2. How large is the room? As a rule of thumb, the bigger the room, the better your recording will be. On that same note, you want to look at the dimensions of the room you use; a perfectly square room will produce a subpar recording when compared to a large, rectangular room. A square room builds up standing waves, leading to an off-balance mixing and recording process. Of course, a larger room not only gives better space for the sound to travel favorably but also gives

you more room for necessary equipment and instruments.

3. How much noise is produced in and around the room? Can you hear your family down the hall or the traffic outside? Is your microphone picking up the sound of your air conditioner or your neighbor mowing his lawn? For the best recording experience, a room should be as quiet as possible, with very little noise filtering into the room.

4. How many surfaces are in the room? Any room with large amounts of hard, reflective surfaces will work against you during recording. Avoid a room with floor-to-ceiling windows and mirrors, or a room with lots of marble or exposed concrete. The exception to this rule is that hardwood flooring is desirable, especially when compared to carpet that will dampen and muffle your sound. Consider how many surfaces are in the room; a kitchen would be a terrible place to record, just by the amount and diversity of objects and surfaces in the room.

Acoustics and Sound-Treatment

Chances are your house probably didn't come with a ready-made space for a home recording studio. Unless you are super lucky or have a house with a recording studio space built into it, you will likely have to find a space and give it a sound treatment.

What Does Sound-Treatment Do?

Every space or building will have sound reflection, resonance, and reverberation. Especially in a recording atmosphere, these need to be properly regulated for your equipment to do its best work. **Reflection** comes from the types of surfaces that the sound waves bounce off. With hard, shiny surfaces, sound waves are reflected back from numerous angles and bounce back unevenly to your recording equipment. It can also add to the reverb coming through your recording. This will throw your sound off, and while some types of editing will help reduce the impact of the imbalance, it is better to resolve the problem at the source.

Resonance creates its own set of problems in recording. When recording, a natural level of frequency resonance is desirable. A room with too much resonance can create a "boomy" sound quality. This comes from too many surfaces amplifying the frequency of the sound waves and creating that "boom" or distorted quality when it comes time to record.

Finally, **reverberation** impacts your recording when too many sound waves come together all at once, creating an undesirable echo. If you go into a room, clap your hands, and get a tin-like echoing sound back, your room has too much reverb. Too much reverb can also contribute to sound decay, making your recordings muddy and busy in all the wrong ways.

Methods of Sound-Treatment

Acoustic Foam

Acoustic foam is often the go-to method for sound treatment but be careful; they are cleverly marketed as an overall problem solver, but this isn't the reality. You have likely seen acoustic foam in someone's home recording studio at some point, with its egg-crate shape. Acoustic foam is ideal for absorbing high frequencies, but in the majority of home studios, it's the low frequencies you need to concern yourself with. While some novice producers might cover their walls in acoustic foam, it is best used in areas where the higher frequencies appear to gather, depending on the layout of your room.

Acoustic Panels

Acoustic panels can sometimes be made of the same type of foam, but instead of looking like an egg carton, these will be flat. The type of foam focuses on absorbing higher frequencies and helps to reduce reverb in the room, which will help reduce the echo in your recording.

Bass Traps

Bass traps keep lower-end frequencies from piling up in the corners of your room. These low-end frequencies can create a deepened booming sound, so having bass traps arranged in the corners of your room can regulate this range of frequency. Typically, a bass trap is made from porous material, such as foams and rigid fiberglass. Depending on the type of material you're using, bass traps can also be effective in absorbing both high and mid frequencies in these corners.

Ceiling Clouds

While having a high ceiling can sometimes be an attractive acoustic feature in a room, sometimes you need to bring that ceiling a little lower. Ceiling clouds are panels that hang horizontally from the ceiling. They control just how high your frequencies are traveling. These can be made from a variety of materials ranging from metal to foam to fiberglass, and they are sometimes wrapped in fabric or other materials, both for aesthetic design and sound absorption. Having a ceiling cloud can be an attractive method of controlling the acoustics in the room.

Diffuser Panels

Acoustic panels, bass traps, and ceiling clouds are all great methods of *absorbing* sound, but sometimes, it is better to diffuse the sound through the room. This is particularly helpful in a room with an echo needing to be dampened rather than flattened. Instead of creating a dead room, diffusion keeps a live sound through the room and recording. Diffusers are made of all kinds of materials, but the key is that they are very three-dimensional. Lots of sound absorption methods are flat panels. Remember back in the day when musicians would put egg cartons all over the walls where they recorded? This shape helps to diffuse sound better (Although I do not recommend egg cartons for diffusion and absorption, there is research that indicates that a couple of mattresses pushed up against the wall work better than a few dozen egg cartons when it comes to sound treatment.) and when it is set up properly, it can be a great compliment to sound-absorbing room treatments.

Fiberglass Insulation

Sound bleed between rooms can be a major issue in any studio; whether it is hearing people in a neighboring room, or needing to prevent sound from escaping your studio, this creates the need for soundproofing. Fiberglass insulation is a great solution to absorbing these soundwaves, no matter in which direction they are traveling.

These sheets of insulation come in multiple varieties of thickness. A thick sheet will absorb long waves of bass, but if you are only able to grab some thinner sheets, setting them up with a small gap between the panel and the wall will absorb those lower sounds. If you have extra, they can even be arranged in the corners of the room to do the same job as a bass trap.

Helmholtz Resonators

If there is too much resonance in your room, a Helmholtz Resonator could be the solution you need. These are usually spherical in shape, with a small hole in the top protruding from a short neck, which helps to collect this resonance. These work by absorbing frequencies like their own. They are offered in a variety of sizes to collect a range of frequencies.

Setting Up Your Studio

Now that you know what you can use to absorb and diffuse sound, you need to know how to arrange them. Once you have chosen the room you will be working in, you will need a place for your desk where your computer and other equipment will go. This shouldn't be centered in the room, but rather position it slightly off-center, and facing a shorter wall.

In an ideal setup, you will have at least two studio monitors. These should be placed at the corners and in front of your desk setup. The key is for the monitors to be facing where you will be sitting, as well as positioned away from your wall. Having the speakers up against the wall will alter your sound and potentially create more low bass frequencies. There should be a good amount of space between the monitor and your wall to give you a better sound overall. Test your positioning until you get the best sound quality; this will make an incredible difference in your editing, mixing, and mastering.

Once you have your positioning set, you will have a better idea of the sound reflection in the room. This is where you can get into the sound-treatment of your room. Every room will be different. Too much sound coming in or out of the room will need soundproofing. Large amounts of bass will require putting bass traps in your corners. High ceilings with extreme acoustics benefit from ceiling clouds. From there, it is about choosing the best sound absorption and diffusion for your budget.

In my experience, once you are standing in the middle of your room with a pile of panels and your adhesive, it is easy to become over-excited and want to start sticking things up. Slow down, measure, and mark your positions so that you know right away if something is out of place. I tend to start with my corners. Setting your bass traps first lets you see how much space you have to work within your room. There is no set formula for where your diffusion and absorption panels should go. It is entirely dependent on the type of equipment you will be working with, the shape and size of the room, and your setup within the room. Each time you put up a strip of paneling, test your sound quality again to see where your sound is heading. Some like to set up their absorption panels first, then add their diffusers over top. There is no requirement for how you set up your room, but you must regularly assess your sound quality.

CHAPTER 3

EQUIPMENT

———————◄O►———————

Audio Interface

Your audio interface is the hardware that connects your gear to your computer so that the recording information can be accessed by your DAW software. It typically looks like a box where you can connect your microphone and other gear. The box has cables that then connect to your computer, bringing the sound information through. It isn't always technically necessary considering the existence of USB microphones that allow you to record directly to your computer, but an audio interface will increase your sound quality, depending on the kind of sound you're looking to produce. More advanced audio interface boxes will give you higher sonic conversion quality, as well as more plug-in options. Lower-end audio interfaces still offer good sound quality, but they will provide only a few plug-in spaces for your equipment.

Cables

Eventually, your studio will have what seems like hundreds of cables, but to start, there are three cables that are necessary when you are first setting up your studio. You will need one long XLR cable for your microphone, and two shorter cables for your monitors. Before running out to purchase your cables, double-check your stereo output is in XLR; if it isn't, it will likely need TRS cables instead.

These cables can sometimes get expensive, but you get what you pay for when it comes to the quality of the cord; if you can't afford the top-quality cords, get the best ones that you can afford.

Digital Audio Workstation (DAW)

Your audio interface hardware works hand in hand with your digital audio workstation, also referred to as your DAW. The DAW is the software that your recorded sounds from your audio interface are imported to be edited, mixed, mastered, and recorded. There is a great selection of DAW software on the market that can provide you with a wide range of flexibility. Of course, it depends on how much you are willing to spend, as well as your skill level and what you want to achieve.

Headphones

There are two types of headphones you will want to have available in a studio setting. The first is a set of closed-back headphones used during the tracking process. They offer better isolation but tend to have lower sound quality. These should be prioritized if finances are limited while you set up your studio. The second is a set of open-back headphones, which offer optimized sound quality for the mixing process but provide less noise isolation.

Because most headphones come with short cables, an extension cable is recommended, so you will be able to move about the room without risking jerking the cord and causing damage. If you do opt for an extension cord for your headphones, do yourself a favor and don't go for the cheapest option. Cheap headphone extension cords are infamous for atrocious signal issues due to the amount of movement they tend to go through, so in this case, buy the best that you can afford.

Laptop/Computer

These days, most people have a laptop or computer at their disposal. While you can have a computer optimized for music production, just about any computer or laptop will give you the capacity to at least get started. This will give you a place to record, as well as give you access to editing, mixing, and recording software, otherwise known as your DAW. If you already have a laptop or computer, do not run out to replace it for the best of the best. If you have a way to input what you record, a reasonable level of sound output, and it can run the software you need, whatever you have will be fine for the time being.

MIDI Keyboard

A midi keyboard allows your sound-producing electronics to communicate with each other. MIDI is an acronym, standing for Musical Instrument Digital Interface. A MIDI keyboard does not produce any sound on its own. Think of it as a musical translator, letting your keyboards and other electronic instruments communicate with your computer in a way that can be understood. When you connect your electronic instrument to your MIDI, which is connected to the computer, messages related to what you are doing on the said instrument will pass through the MIDI. The MIDI will describe what is happening to the computer so that it will be understood and recorded.

A MIDI does so much more than just help your computer understand your fancy fingers on your synthesizer. It can also be a powerful tool that helps you mix and edit your work. Both from the keyboard itself, and the software, you can alter all kinds of sounds, effects, and even change what instrument it sounds like you're playing, even if you're just hitting some keys on the board. A MIDI keyboard is an essential component for anyone who is doing work with electronic recording.

Microphone

Not all microphones are made equal. There are several types of microphones to consider when choosing how to record in your setup.

Microphone Types

Condenser

A condenser mic is a great option for vocals if the sound pressure levels don't rise too high. The diaphragm found in these microphones is a thin, conductive coil sitting close to a metal backplate. The diaphragm needs to be powered by batteries, USB, or a phantom power source. The plates are superior to coiled diaphragm microphones because they do not rely on the movement of the coils and make them more precise in the recording studio. The downside is that they tend to be more fragile than the other microphones.

Dynamic

A dynamic mic is perfect for capturing high-pressure sound, like the booming volumes of a guitar amp, without having to worry about excessive distortion. The diaphragm is a magnetic metal coil which makes them fantastic for high and low sound pressure levels (SPL) and capturing a clear and reliable recording. The dynamic mic is versatile in its usage, making it an ideal microphone in live performances and the recording studio.

Ribbon

Ribbon mics used to be the standard of recording, particularly in radio. The diaphragm is a long, pleated strip of thin metal, usually aluminum, connected to electronic leads at each end of the pleat. Two magnets sit on each end, helping to conduct the vibration and record the sounds we produce. The ribbon mic provides a warm sound with a vintage feel and can make for great vocal recording. They make good mics for high frequencies, which over time have become far more durable than their previous counterparts.

Diaphragm Sizes

A diaphragm is a form of the membrane inside the microphone that helps to pick up and transfer sound. It responds to the variations of sound pressure by vibrating the membrane, converting the acoustic sounds we produce in the studio into electronic energy that is recorded for use. The size of the diaphragm impacts the quality of this energy in recording.

Small

A small-diaphragm mic is sometimes called a pencil mic because of its long, thin design. If you're seeking to record a higher sound pressure, a smaller diaphragm is preferred. These mics are designed to be sturdy with a stiff diaphragm design. The design can present other issues such as the stiffness causing the small diaphragm microphone to be less sensitive to sound unless it's at the higher end of pressure. They can also be prone to higher amounts of internal noise from the microphone.

Medium

A medium-sized diaphragm is sometimes referred to as a hybrid because it can combine the sound capture characteristics of both a small and a large-diaphragm microphone. They can still capture the sensitivity to the sound pressure and the warmth of a large-diaphragm mic while also handling the higher sound pressures of a small diaphragm. The medium diaphragm microphone has gained popularity in both studio settings and live settings, but if you already have a small and a large-diaphragm microphone, then you can safely take a pass on a medium.

Large

A larger diaphragm means higher sensitivity to sound. These diaphragms respond better to variations in sound, but they need to have a regulated volume during recording. Otherwise, the higher ends of volume can cause it to create distortion and an inconsistent bass boost effect. However, if you are

MUSIC PRODUCTION 2022+ EDITION

regulating the distance, and thus the volume of the instrument or voice being recorded, a large-diaphragm microphone can be useful in an all-purpose sense in a recording studio setting.

Polar Patterns

Cardioid

The cardioid microphone is by far the most popular microphone to use in both recordings and live settings. This comes from the fact that it is a front-facing sound capture, limiting noise pick up from behind the microphone. Wherever the microphone is pointed is the primary area where the sound will be picked up, reducing ambient and residual sound from the surrounding room or venue. If you are new to recording, be sure to take your time to test angles on your cardioid microphone to find the best positioning. If your mic is not angled properly, it can add coloration and other distortion to the mic sound.

Figure-8

This sound pattern is typically found in ribbon microphones, as well as some large diaphragm condenser mics. The sound is easily picked up in the front of the microphone, as well as behind it, but the sounds to the sides of the microphone are rejected. This is ideal for stereo recording or recording multiple instruments at the same time.

Hyper/Super-Cardioid

While a cardioid microphone will reject the sound coming from behind the microphone, a hyper-cardioid or super-cardioid microphone needs to be carefully angled with its back end in noise dead zones. They have the same front-focused directionality as the cardioid, but with a slightly narrower field of sensitivity in comparison. This makes them great for recording in untreated rooms and recording louder instruments, but this narrowed field is where the difficulty comes in with picking up back-end noise; the noise rejection from the back is quite compromised, more so with hyper-cardioid mics over super-cardioid microphones.

Multipattern

These microphones offer versatility that you don't often get in most microphones. Flip a switch, and you can adjust what kind of polar pattern you're using depending on the room you're in or the desired effect. Some also let you change the polarity by switching the mic head, but this does come with a downside; if you are not careful, you could potentially damage the diaphragm or the internal circuitry that gives it such great versatility. While a multi-pattern microphone is great, all the additional moving parts can make them more difficult to upkeep if you do not have good storage and aren't careful with their handling.

Omnidirectional

An omnidirectional microphone is great if you're recording in a room with phenomenal acoustics, and you want to pick up all the nuanced, natural sounds that you can. This type of microphone picks up everything from all directions. This also poses some issues; every sound in the vicinity is collected by the microphone, so if you are recording in an area that is not sound-treated, anything that you would prefer not to be picked up will find its way into your recording. The same thing applies to live venues. Lots of background noise will be picked up by your microphone, which may distort the sound you are hoping to produce during your performance. This lack of noise rejection makes an omnidirectional microphone a poor choice for loud venues and an inadequately sound-treated studio.

Shotgun

Shotgun microphones, otherwise referred to as Line and Gradient microphones are typically used in film and theater settings because their design is good for picking up sound at a distance. In the recording studio, shotgun mics are useful for recording a choir, cymbals, or any other group. The tubular design is excellent for rejecting noise to the sides and gathering the sound from the front and back at large distances.

Microphone Stand

If you're new to music production or recording in general, it's easy to think that all microphone stands are made equal. This isn't the case. If you have ever spent time looking up different microphone stands, you've probably seen that they can be expensive. Getting something that is adequately sturdy is ideal for a beginner studio. Going cheap is a great way to send you diving to the floor to catch your expensive microphone before it collides with the floor. Do yourself a favor and spend time going through reviews. Choose the best quality stand within your budget so that you do not potentially sacrifice your more expensive recording equipment.

Microphone stands come in six main varieties:

Desktop

Desktop stands are ideal for podcasting and bedroom studio recording. They are small and compact and the best choice for small recording spaces. They are typically a simple round base, but sometimes they are a small tripod that easily sits on the desktop. The height is usually comfortable when used in a seated position.

Low Profile

These stands are less often used for vocals and are instead used for adding microphones to kickdrums, guitar cabinets, and other lower recording needs.

Overhead

These are best for use with shotgun microphones and are easily the largest and most expensive microphone stands. These are ideally used to set up above a drum kit or a group of people who will be singing in chorus.

Round Base

The round base microphone stand is what you most often see a performer singing into on stage. This is because the round base is significantly harder to trip over, and it takes up much less space in comparison to tripod stands.

Tripod

The tripod stand is an alternative to the round base and is good for general-purpose recording. They are one of the most common microphones stands used, but they can take up quite a bit of room in a smaller recording space. When room space is limited, tripods can also pose a tripping hazard, but in a room with a reasonable amount of space, they are perfectly fine.

Tripod Boom

A tripod boom stand is useful if you need more reach, depending on where you have your microphone stand setup, and how much room you have available. A tripod boom is quite large, but helpful if you're reaching over instruments or other equipment.

Monitor Speakers

While a good portion of your editing process can be done on headphones, using studio monitors, the traditional method of mixing, is highly recommended. These are different from standard speakers in that they offer a flatter, more neutral sound that can make the mixing process much easier. Typical consumer speakers tend to have enhancements and tweaks that alter the listening experience of the consumer. Some speakers have preset treble adjustments, while others offer a heavier bass sound, which does not pair well with mixing and editing. Having a couple of studio monitors can make a difference when you mix and edit your work so that you get the most accurate depiction of your work.

Phantom Power Source

A phantom power source is necessary when working with condenser microphones, given that they need a consistent power supply for their electronic diaphragms. If you are using a dynamic or USB microphone, you won't need a phantom power source. A phantom power source uses a direct current to ensure there is a constant power supply to prevent cutting and other issues in your condenser microphone. In many cases, you can get an audio interface that will act as a phantom power source, so you may not have to get an additional supply source.

Pop Filter

A pop filter, among the many other forms of microphone filters, isn't technically necessary in a home studio, but they do go a long way in improving the audio quality. Pop filters tend to be fairly cheap circular mesh filters that are set in front of your microphone. They reduce popping coming from the pronunciation of the letters 'p' and 'b,' and can help you to maintain a good distance from your microphone so that you don't end up with uneven bass boosts and other issues in your recording.

CHAPTER 4

SONGWRITING AND CONSTRUCTION

———————◆O◆———————

Song construction is key in creating a hit song. Song structure provides a formula for creating music so that we might be the producer behind the next summer smash or the song playing at everyone's wedding. This is a combination of structuring the instrumental track and writing the lyrical story so that it complements the track. Songwriting is an important component in the construction of a song. There must be a complementary relationship between the music and lyrics as you develop your song.

Songwriting is where the magic begins. This is the portion of the production process when the writing of the music and lyrics happens. Each instrument adds another layer to the song, the lyrical story growing over the music. The method of songwriting differs between every artist. Some are classic guitar-and-notepad writers, working up the lyrics with a melody. Others might prefer to be working at a piano or recording snippets of lyrics on recorders. Often, a drumbeat is the beginning of the songwriting process, building the foundation of the song from the ground up.

Breaking Down the Sections of a Song

Intro

The intro to your song is key to grabbing your listener. It might be a unique sound or effect on your vocals or instrumentals or a catchy beat. The key to the intro is to create something to captivate the listener that can be built on. The intro of the song should be a good indication of what the song will be like; is it a tear-jerker that will get into the listeners' emotions, or are you pumping them up for an amazing night? The energy of the song should be present in the intro. The key to the intro is that it can be built on. No matter how simple or intricate the introduction to the song is, it is simply a prelude to what you want your listener to be getting into.

A good intro is a key to preventing the listener from skipping past your song. There are plenty of factors that might lead a listener to skip a song; maybe they have just heard it, and do not like the style of the music, or they do not know the song. No matter the reason they are skipping, our goal as producers and songwriters is to hook that listener in and keep them all the way through the song. According to a study done by Music Machinery, a listener will skip a song approximately fourteen times in an hour. Twenty-four percent of those skips happen within the first *five seconds*, while thirty-five percent of those skips come within the first thirty seconds of the song. Making sure that the introduction of your song can hook that listener is crucial to get them past that 30-second mark and transform them into regular fans and listeners. Even then, there is a forty-eight percent chance of that song being skipped before it's over. A great intro to your song will improve your chances. An intro will typically last for four bars and can either be made up of the music found in the body (or verses) of the song or something unique to that section of the song altogether if it blends nicely with the change in music.

Verse

Your verse is where your song should begin to open up. A good verse is typically under a minute long. It provides support to your intended chorus. This is where your story develops, giving the context of the song and its intent with every verse that plays. Though verses are broken up by the bridge, the chorus, and the hook, the music of the verses is often what ties the song together, giving it a consistent sound. The rhythm of the music and tempo of the lyrics should stay consistent between verses so that there is some level of predictability for someone who may be trying to sing along. It is important to remember not to overwhelm the track's verse sections with the music if you intend for the music to be sung over. The lyrics should take precedence allowing the music of the verse to support the energy of the story being told.

Pre-chorus/Bridge

The Pre-chorus gives a bit of space between the verse and the chorus. Sometimes, this might be referred to as the "Lift" of the song. The pre-chorus does not always include lyrics. It is usually a shorter section where the music picks up in intensity or feeling as it moves from the verse into the bridge or chorus. Think of it as the anticipation builder to the chorus by building up the tempo, the volume, and the overall tension as it drives you into the power of the chorus. It is not found in every song but is a common piece in rock and heavier music.

The **Bridge** works similarly to the pre-chorus, in that it builds anticipation and tension. There is usually some tie-in to the verses as it throws you into the energy of the chorus offering familiarity as it lifts the listener. The bridge doesn't necessarily have to sound like the verses though; while it is nice to keep an element that ties it in, a bridge tends to catch the listener off guard, sometimes with rogue lines and a change-up in the musical elements to keep a listener hooked.

Chorus/Hook

The **chorus** is the big bang of the song and should typically be the climax of the song. If it's an upbeat, energetic song, the chorus should be the peak of that energy. In a slower song, the pinnacle of emotion should be in the chorus. In rock songs, the chorus is where the mosh pit should be rocking the hardest. This means the energy of the song should build to the chorus.

The **hook** is often found in the chorus and takes the form of a line or two that repeat. This is usually the part of the song that reflects the song title and is the "earworm" that gets stuck in your head. Some might also call the hook a refrain, but they ultimately come down to the same thing; a few catchy lines that stick in the listener's mind, hopefully inspiring them to listen to your song over and over again.

Break

Not every song comes with a break, but some benefit from it. A break is a space in the song that allows for instrumentals to shine and are sometimes complemented with spoken interludes or vocalizations. A break is great for transitioning into a new section of music, or when the song's storyline takes a different direction. It can also help tie in other songs from the album, or past albums.

Outro

The outro does exactly what it suggests; it leads the song out and brings the song to a close. An outro might be instrumental, might be a repeated refrain, or might come to a sharp halt. No matter how you choose to bring the song to an end, it should bring the song to a close.

Building Your Song Structure

Song structure gathers the sections of songs that we've just gone over and arranged them within their formula. There isn't a single formula that works over the other, just varying formulas for success for different types of songs and genres. Ultimately, the song structure of your choice comes down to what you're hoping to accomplish in terms of your listening experience. This comes down to a few things; the story within or behind your song, and the emotions you want to get across. Even then, there's no set rule pattern. Do what comes naturally. The more natural it feels to you, the better it translates to a listener's ear.

Song structure can happen in two ways; some producers start with music first, knowing the feeling and emotional connections you want the audience to hear, but still needing a story to be told over it. Figuring out the music that will go into the various sections can give you the freedom to piece your formula together when the time comes. Other producers build their story and lyrics first. Instead of finding the melody and tempo, they work through the story set up and build the music around it. Chances are that each song you write will go about this process differently until you find your preferred way to create your masterpieces.

Defining the Plot of Your Song

Sometimes, you are working from an already established mental idea of what your song's story will be. It might be from personal experience or inspired by a scene or recurring theme in your life. Longer, more in-depth stories tend to benefit from a song structure with plenty of verses, where the chorus is present, but otherwise not the focus. In a woeful, heartbroken song, a wilting lament may fit better in a song with shorter verses, and more focus on the bridge and chorus. The ultimate goal is to do the storyline justice by learning how to maximize your usage of every line to tell a clear story between three to four minutes. While it might sound daunting, as you develop as a songwriter, you learn to trim unnecessary drama and filter it from your lyrics.

Feeling the Story

Once you know what your story is about, you want to consider what you want your listener to feel while wrapped up in your song. Your music and storyline should tie together cohesively; moments of pain are expressed in soft, lingering notes or powerful, howling rhythms. An upbeat party anthem will come with an accelerated tempo and rhythms that are easy to move to and inspire about fist-pumping and jumping in the air.

Rhythm and Melody

Being aware of both rhythm and melody can make a difference in the quality of the music on your track. Having a good **rhythm** to your track will set the pace of your song, whereas the **melody** will determine the quality of the music itself. It can make it easier to consider melody as the tune to your track, whereas the rhythm sets the tempo and timing to the track. Both need to work together to create a quality track.

Rests and Intervals

Never underestimate the power of silence within a song! Rests and intervals are a great tool in building the anticipation and energy in a song. Going back a little over a decade, *Misery Business* as released by Paramore is a great example of the proper use of the **rest**. Just a moment's pause between the verse and chorus takes the high energy and angst of the verse into a powerful explosion of energy as we go into the chorus. Rests are a great way to break up a song, especially if you're hoping to add drama or make a slight interval change. **Intervals** are the change in pitch from one note to the other. Using the right intervals can help your music rise and fall, controlling the intensity and energy of the song. Combining rests and intervals can act as an auditory staircase, moving up and down and leading your listener where you want them to be.

Prosody

Prosody refers to the way your lyrics are sung. Singing and speaking focus on different areas of stress, pitch, rhythm, and intonation. A song with good prosody blends and weaves the vocal artist's voice with the music and pays attention to the way the lyrics follow the rhythm and melody. A common mistake for beginner songwriters is to make the vocals match the music almost exactly. Instead, prosody engages complementary rhythms and melodies in the song and lyrics and finds a happy balance between the two.

Song Structure Formula

A common method of describing song structure follows an A-B-C method: A represents your verses, B represents your chorus, and C represents your bridge. While other sections may be placed between these three, these are the main ones used when speaking of song structure formulas.

The "ABABCB" Song Structure

One of the most common song structures seen across genres is the ABABCB, or verse, chorus, verse, chorus, bridge, chorus. This formula lends itself to effective songwriting because it engages the most important aspects of what attracts the listener. The two verses allow for the story to be built, without taking over the entire song. The repetition of the chorus, typically including the hook, allows for it to be the earworm and predictable portion of the song that everyone will likely remember, even if they forget the words to the verses. The added bridge between choruses at the end helps alter the energy of the song. It also offers the changeup in a catchy way. The bridge can create tension or anticipation before exploding back into the chorus. The bridge can turn the energy level up on the song so that the listener ends the song on a dopamine-fueled musical high. In terms of timing, this formula builds to allow for a traditional three-to-four-minute song without much thought or effort required from producers or songwriters.

The ABABCB structure isn't the only one used, even if it is widely popular. Often writers will use subtle variations on this structure depending on their goal. A story-driven song might have more focus on verses, such as AABAABCB. A song with shorter verses or a more powerful chorus might run along the lines of ABABCBB. A song that seeks to focus more on instrumentals might find that ABAB, AABA, or AACA highlights the instrumentals more, especially when looking at high-energy electronic mixes.

The point here is that, while the ABABCB structure works, and is highly popular for a reason, there isn't a single way to go about structuring your song. The structure will be highly dependent on the genre, as well as your personal goals for the journey your song takes a listener on. The popular structure is helpful to beginning songwriters, but feel free to experiment to create your ideal musical experience.

Other Useful Song Structures

Verse-Verse-Bridge-Verse

This structure is not as commonly used, but it can still be functional in popular music. This style is effective when combined with a repeating refrain after each verse and relies heavily on a strong hook. It can sometimes make for a shorter song, but if your hook is strong enough, the length of the song becomes inconsequential, provided it is done well.

Verse-Chorus-Verse-Chorus

Like the ABABCB structure, the Verse-Chorus repetition used to be far more popular than it is now. This song structure allows for clear and effective storytelling, as well as building engagement for the listener through a repeating chorus or refrain.

Verse-Prechorus-Chorus-Verse-Prechorus-Chorus

Adding a pre-chorus can make a world of difference to the song. The pre-chorus gives a bit of anticipation and some subtle mention of what is to come in the chorus itself and can add to the drive of the song. A pre-chorus is a tension builder before the big release of the chorus.

Finding Your Inner Lyricist

Once you understand the layout for your song, the fun part starts with the writing of lyrics! Songwriting can be intimidating given all the music out there; how do you come up with something original? Technically, you don't. We all know the common themes in most music, falling in love, falling out of love, professing your love and devotion, singing about your family, about trauma, hanging out, and having fun with your friends. We write about these unforgettable moments good and bad because they are relatable. They are consequences of being human and experiencing human interaction.

Writing the lyrics of a song is hardly different from writing a short story. Most tips for writing an effective story can be effective when writing out the lyrics to your song. Focus on the message of your song, and what you have to say. Think of an elevator pitch; if you can't sum up the story of your song in the time it takes to get on and off an elevator, there's too much going on in the story. The following tips are here to help you focus your craft and improve the quality of your lyrics.

Don't Be Scared of Revision

It is common for beginner writers to be frustrated that the first couple of drafts of their song didn't turn out the way they thought it would. Maybe you want something more profound, maybe the message isn't coming across the way you wanted to, or maybe the flow is all wrong with the music. That's totally normal for the songwriting process.

Take a little comfort from the fact that many professional lyricists regularly do dozens of rounds of revisions before the lyrics are where they want them to be when recording.

Revision isn't just finding new words to say the same thing. Revision adjusts the message of the song, the rhyme scheme, the words used, and replaces ideas that were not working in the song. There might be a line you absolutely love that just doesn't fit the song; set it aside, it might do well in another song or could be slightly reworded to fit later down the road. Ultimately, revision is your friend. It's rare to have a perfectly written song on the first try, so give yourself a break if things are not coming out the way you want them to right away.

Avoid Overuse of Metaphor and Simile

This is where the writing premise of "show, don't tell" comes in. Yes, having poetic elements in the song can bring it to life, but if every other line is some metaphor or simile, it gets old quickly. Your message becomes blurred under all of these illusions to your story, without directly telling the story. We want to know what is going on, not just the surface of what we might interpret to be happening in the song.

Think of metaphor as the seasoning to your meal; a little bit of cayenne can add a delightful bit of spice to a dish while bringing out the flavors of the dish. Drowning the dish in cayenne is overpowering, and you lose the flavor of the meal. Using simile and metaphor in your song is the same. Focus on telling the story of the song, and add dashes of metaphor to it, rather than having it run the whole process. The story should be told easily and conversationally like you are speaking to a friend as you perform your song.

The same also applies to the use of cliché. Artists that use cliché in their work typically already have an established following and do not have anything to prove. While an occasional cliché can be forgiven, writing songs full of them will drive away from the audience. If you are struggling with clichés in your writing, try focusing more on imagery and storytelling.

Play With Rhyme

Songs typically follow some type of rhyme scheme. The thing is, it does not have to be perfect, and it can vary through the song. Play with different rhyming patterns, and test what comes naturally to you as you write. Dive into poetry books and examine the variety of rhyme schemes for inspiration. Experiment with the patterns, the types of rhyming, and where you place your rhyme. A rhyme does not have to always land at the end of the line.

Another area where rhyme can work against you is if you are trying to force a rhyme scheme. Always remember that when you're trying to force lines to work, they tend to stand out as exactly that: not working. When you are struggling, it can help to step back and listen to the music as it is at that moment. Keep your storyline in mind, and see what lines come naturally and easily. If nothing is coming to you at that point, walk away from it, and approach it later when you have had time to separate yourself from the frustrating rhyme scheme.

Reference Songwriters You Respect

When you're struggling with inspiration, or you find that everything you have written seems to miss the mark, it can help to turn to pros in the business. Choose a few artists who have a style you'd like to emulate and read through their lyrics. Specifically, *read* them, *do not* listen to the song. Getting the rhythms and melodies stuck in your head makes it far more likely that you will accidentally copy their work.

As you read through the lyrics, look at the way they arrange their story. Look for repetition, imagery, and storytelling tactics that they use. What kinds of signatures can you find, and what do you want to translate into your work? Sometimes all it takes is catching a line that sparks inspiration! Just like a writer should always be reading to hone their craft, a lyricist should be paying attention to the work of other lyricists and learning from them.

CHAPTER 5

RECORDING

---◀O▶---

In the early days of recording, the process was much easier, and as such, much faster. The band would pile into their studio, get set up with their instruments, and with no more than 1-2 microphones, they would simply play the song they'd written and practiced. Most times, they would finish the job within a few takes, and that was that; they'd just recorded the song with plenty of time to get home for dinner.

While the process might have been delightfully easy, we also know the difference in sound quality that we find in modern recording. We use a multitude of microphones and now use multi-track recording. Each instrument or layer to the music is recorded individually, done with the ideal microphone for the job. While this takes far more time, there are some distinct advantages. First, each instrument can be individually edited for the ideal sound. This is not possible with a single-track recording; if an engineer wanted to adjust the sound, they would have to do it for the entire track. The second advantage lies in the fact that, instead of hauling a whole band into the studio to get the track over with, each instrument is recorded individually. With the progression of the internet in the modern-day, this means being able to work with musicians from all over the globe, and everyone can work on their ideal schedule. If you choose to work on your own, it means being able to have your hands on every instrument, much like Dave Grohl did when creating the mixtape for the very first Foo Fighters demo.

Recording Fundamentals

As with anything, there is not a single method on the recording process; each artist, producer, and engineer will have their take on the way a song is recorded. However, the following steps are an easy place to start and can help you build your recording routine while you figure out your ideal method.

Set a Base Track

There are a few ways you can go about this, and it's all going to depend on the person. Some might turn to a metronome to set their tempo, but not every artist is good at recording by rhythmic ticking. A more common method in modern days is to set a drum loop to record over. This gives a more defined rhythm to follow, between bass, snare, and tops that can be added in to refine the information the musician is working with.

Another helpful method for recording is a scratch track. This provides a guide to the musician, essentially a draft copy of the music that can be recorded over. Each piece of the track gets steadily replaced as the musician(s) record the cleaner version of each instrument. By the end, the entire scratch track gets replaced, or "scratched," by the better recordings.

Record Your Rhythms

In my experience, recording your rhythm section first provides the blueprint to the song. Other areas like melody and harmony fit together better when you know what the rhythm is going to be because you follow the drumline for maintaining rhythm and tempo. In acoustic songs, it is perfectly reasonable to set the rhythm with a guitar or bass since percussion tends to be limited in acoustic styles.

Add Your Harmonies

This is where you will fill out the sound a little more. When your rhythms are established, adding chord progressions will give the track body. This can be done with guitars, piano, synthesizers, brass instruments, whatever it is that you have in mind.

Bring in the Melody

Establish how you're going to lead your melody. Typically, this will be with vocals, or sometimes a lead guitar. Once you have the core of your melody down, bring in other instrumentation to subtly build the melody. This area is easy to overdo. Be critical of how much you add because you do not want the track to be too busy.

Add a Little Flavor

Once you have all the core pieces of your song down, this is the point where you can add fillers to the sound. This could be filling in with piano or various types of percussion or adding background vocals. This is also where you can add electronic components like sound samples and other effects. Be careful to not add every sound and sample under the sun. Be choosy and find what best fits your song.

Tricks for Recording Instruments

Acoustic Guitar

Recording an acoustic guitar is not for the faint of heart. For all of the lovely simplicity of an acoustic guitar, it is a complex instrument in the recording sense. The plucking of the strings, the tapping of the frets and the soundboard muting the strings with your hand, and the squeak of the strings as your fingers move along the strings all get picked up by the mic. Sometimes, these additional sounds make a wonderful recording with an omnidirectional condenser mic set up. If you are going that route, the mic should be about a foot away from the guitar, pointing roughly in the direction of the twelfth fret. Depending on your room's acoustics, this might need a little bit of experimentation with angles and distance.

When you want a cleaner sound, you need to trade up your approach. This leaves you with two main options. If you are hoping not to plug in for the recording process, you can put stereo recording to use; two microphones angled inwards toward your guitar. This will give you a fuller, deeper sound than with a single microphone. If you are willing to plug into an acoustic D1 direct box, you will find a cleaner recording than a single mic or stereo setup.

Drums

If you like a challenge, recording drums straight off the drum kit is one of the hardest things to do, particularly from a home studio. First off, drums are *so loud*. If you have neighbors and play your drums in a space that is not noise-containing, I can guarantee that your neighbors aren't thrilled. Unless, of course, you're lucky enough to have some hardcore music enthusiasts as neighbors. Beyond this, recording drums for your track means needing a lot of space for equipment, both the drum kit, and all the arms for various microphones, cables for the input channels, and more. Of course, there is also needing the space for creating an open, acoustic recording experience. While it is not impossible, it takes a lot of testing out the various locations for the microphones and related equipment, as well as figuring out the best location for the drum kit.

Each piece of the drum kit needs its own mic setup. In all honesty, the topic of properly setting up a recording arrangement for drums could be a book all on its own, but some basics can give you a foundation to work with:

- **Hi-Hats** - Use a small diaphragm condenser mic located nearby, directed towards the hi-hat
- **Kick drums** - The best setup on kick drums is two bass mics, one on either side of the drum to pick up the frequencies in stereo.
- **Snare** - Snare drums are best picked up with dynamic mics; one set up above and below the drum to catch the cracking of the impact, as well as the rattle of the snare.
- **Toms** - A good dynamic mic will do the trick, and each tom gets its own mic.
- **Cymbals** - Individual condenser mics are best per set of cymbals.
- **Individual drums** - A good rule of thumb when missing individual drums is to make sure you're positioning the mic downward towards the drumhead from the rim. It should be as close as possible, without being in smacking range of the drumsticks. For best results, the mics should be angled as far as possible from neighboring drums to prevent excessive noise bleeding.

If you want an easier option that can still be physically played, an electronic drum kit will be the best alternative. You must do your due diligence in searching out a good, and I mean *really good* set. The good sets will give you a dynamic sound, and the best ones will even allow each drum piece to record into its own track, making it amazingly easy to edit, all without harassing the whole neighborhood.

The final alternative to recording your drums on a kit is a virtual drum set. By far the most conservative in terms of space, a virtual drum kit is just about as convincing as a true drum set in recording and often sounds even better than a true recording of a drummer on a set. This comes from the fact that virtual drum kits are recorded in top-of-the-line studios by some of the top drummers in the world. Recording from sounds and loops created by the best drummers? It's a sure-fire way to get the best drum sounds possible onto your track.

Electric Guitar/Bass

When you are looking for the perfect studio-quality sound, there is nothing that will compare to putting your mic right up to the amp. Setting up your guitar cabinet means finding yourself a quality ribbon or dynamic mic and experimenting with positioning your amp and mic until you find the ideal positioning. This can mean raising the amp off the floor to minimize the acoustics that will come off the floor, testing angling and distance for both your mic and your amp to minimize reverb and sound reflection off the walls and testing out the best location within the room. The difference when recording bass is that instead of a dynamic or ribbon mic, you want to choose a bass mic. Otherwise, recording bass in this method is barely different than when working with an electric guitar.

If you are in a smaller space and require a quieter method of recording your electric guitar, a direct box may be your best bet. This gives you a way to record directly into your DAW and combine it with an amp simulator to create a virtual electric guitar sound. When recording your bass, you will see a difference in the recording based on your pickups, depending on your style of bass. If you use a passive bass, you will want active DI pickups and vice versa.

The final method of getting your electric guitar recorded onto your track is called reamping. In some ways, this combines the traditional and direct box. With reamping, you get the flexibility and ease of use of an amp simulator, while still getting that straight-from-the-amp sound. Even after you have recorded your track, reamping still gives you the freedom to tweak the tone and rerecord the track you've worked on, without having to pick the guitar or bass back up.

Keyboards

Recording keyboards is beautifully easy for one simple reason; unlike a drum set or an acoustic guitar, the keyboard is already a digital instrument. If you happen to *be* a keyboardist, all you need is a stereo D1 direct box. This will be far easier than attempting to hook up a mic to pick up the sound when played; a keyboard is a high output instrument. When a mic is set up, its sound has a higher chance of cutting out due to the frequencies and output.

If you are not a great keyboardist, a virtual keyboard is far more forgiving. When combined with a MIDI controller, a virtual multi-instrument keyboard allows for better editing over not-so-favorable performances and is far easier to control during the recording process. On top of all that, it's far cheaper than getting yourself a high-end keyboard or piano and great in terms of saving space in a home studio.

What if You're Not Recording with Instruments?

If you're a purely electronic producer or artist, your recording process looks a lot more like tracking. It is straightforward and can be a fairly quick process when you know what you're doing.

Gather Your Sounds

Since recording electronically means creating music out of already existing sound files, go through your resources to gather the sounds that you like for your project. This can come in the form of free or paid sound packs, loops, sounds you've pulled for other songs, or recorded sound that you create on your own. This is one of the most enjoyable areas of song production as an electronic artist, in my opinion. There are all kinds of different sound libraries that you can choose from, and no shortage of material to draw inspiration from.

Once you've gathered the sounds that you like, put them together on your board. This will depend on what kind of board you're using, or if you're hooking it onto a synthesizer or keyboard, a beat pad, or even a software app. No matter where you're recording from, make sure you've got everything arranged to where you want it. Play around with it while you set up, so you can find where you like each sound best, and where it's going to be the most intuitive for use.

Establish Your Beat

Just like with traditional recording, your rhythms are what you're going to build your song over. Think of your beat as your foundation. It does not have to be complicated. It has to be simple, sturdy, and buildable. Do not worry about all the details; those can be added later.

Organize a Simple Structure

Much like your beat, the structure does not have to be complicated. Organizing something simple will help to alleviate headaches down the road. If you already have a decent rhythm and melody structure to work with, you have a visual on your screen that helps to organize the finer details, and you can easily scrap the original structure pieces for more refined and better sounding loops and sounds.

Sound-Design

This is the part that most people enjoy! Play with different loops and sounds, splice loops, and mess around with some knobs and synthesizers. This phase can be highly experimental but can result in incredible tracks. This is also where you can add in filler sounds, and experiment with effects on each area of the track until you feel like you've found your song.

Step Away

While this can be helpful in any type of recording, I find it especially necessary with electronic recording. When you are recording instruments, it can sometimes be easier to be objective about that layer of sound. With electronic recording, it is easy to get lost in the blur of sounds, thoughts, and ideas. I find that, when working on individual tracks, it works best to set yourself a timer for how long you can work on a song. Set an hour aside to play with the track. Then save your file and walk away from it for a day. In the meantime, if the creative juices are flowing, start another timer, set up another track, and repeat as often as you wish.

When you return to the track the next day, you will have a clearer idea of what does and does not work. This gives you some time to come in with new ideas that might have worked well in other tracks and figure out what you are not loving when you originally set it up. Creating some distance between you and the track gives you fresh ears to hear where things might sound too busy, or help you figure out where your track might be lacking. Even in terms of the recorded vocals, you may find lines that do not work the way you want them, or they may need more depth.

Recording Vocals

Recording vocals is often seen as the easy part. Grab a microphone, get a vocalist on it, and hit record. Right? While that may be the gist of the process, there are a few aspects you need to consider to create a top-of-the-line recording, versus a recording that sounds like it was made in the basement.

Foot Noise

It is easy not to think of your feet when you are focused on recording your voice. This means that a vocalist may be shuffling their feet or tapping their foot to the music as they record. The sound gets picked up through the mic stand or the echo in the room. To prevent this, consider getting a shock mount. A shock mount will prevent the footsteps directly around the mic, as well as in the home from registering on the recording.

If you are unsure if you need a shock mount, set your mic to record, and turn up the gain. Move around the microphone stand, or have people walk through the house and listen to the recording. If you are catching the sounds of the footsteps, then you'd benefit from a shock mount.

Popping

Popping comes from how we pronounce 'p' and 'b'. When we use these letters, we push air through our lips in a more pronounced way. We may not notice it as much when we are speaking amongst ourselves, but if you place your hand in front of your mouth while using these letters, you will notice a little push, or pop, of air against your skin. A microphone will pick this little bit of air up in a more defined way, which can bring down the quality of your recording.

There is a simple fix to this issue, pop filters. Of course, you can train yourself as a vocalist to sing at an off-angle from the microphone, but in the case of newer vocalists who have not quite gotten there yet, a pop filter is an easy way to keep that popping from being an issue in the recording.

Room Acoustics

As repeatedly mentioned, the acoustics of the room makes a difference in recording anything, vocals included. If you have not been able to give the room a proper acoustic treatment, there is a solution; not a perfect one, but one that will do the trick until proper acoustic treatment can be done. A reflection filter may be added to the mic stand to help control any echo, reverb, or undesirable reflection. Typically, they curve around the microphone and can be made from a variety of materials. A reflection filter contains the vocalist's voice and has the advantage of blocking other undesirable noise. Even if you do have a well-treated room, it can still benefit the quality of your recording.

Sibilance

Like popping, sibilance comes from the way our mouths pronounce the letters 's' and 'f'. Instead of a popping sound on the mic, these letters produce a hissing sound. There is a simple hack to this problem that does not involve buying filters and other equipment. Attach a pencil to your mic, directly in the middle where you would be singing. This will diffuse the sound, and just like that, you no longer have to fiddle around with the de-esser.

Standing Too Close (or Too Far)

A good amount of the mics commonly used are cardioid mics, which are the standard polar pattern when looking for a good vocal mic. This means that the proximity to the mic makes a difference; if you get within an inch of the diaphragm of the microphone, it picks up the lower-end frequency. The closer you get to the mic the more pronounced this boost becomes. As you move closer and further, this boost responds accordingly. When you listen back to the recording, there will be a rising and fading boost at random, which can be a nightmare for editing.

The solution? Switch to an omnidirectional microphone or set up a pop filter. The pop filter will control your distance from the diaphragm to prevent that boost from being picked up.

CHAPTER 6

EDITING LIKE A PRO

You could be the best recording artist that ever existed, and there will still be points of your recordings that will benefit from some amount of editing. There are five core areas to focus on when editing a track:

- Arrangements
- Comping
- Noise reduction
- Pitch editing
- Time editing

Arrangements

Editing your arrangements means carefully evaluating each track you have recorded for quality and usability. This is where you need to be considering the value of each track recorded. Some tracks may have poor recording quality that no amount of editing or mixing will improve or there are some errors that make the entire track worthless. These tracks can be deleted. There is no point in wasting the memory space on something that can't be used.

Once you go through the individual tracks, it can be helpful to play them together. You can give the entire song an evaluation this way. Some sections might not flow as well as anticipated and could benefit from being switched over to another area of the song or being removed outright. During the playthrough, listen for the areas that seem too busy, or have too much clutter in the sound. Go through these areas and find what can be removed to open up the song, and level out the sound.

Comping

Comping is going through the repeat recordings. If you do three takes on vocals, compare them next to each other to choose the best version of the recording. You won't always find one recording that outshines the others all the way through. In that case, you can create a new track using the best pieces of each recording to create a new overall recording. Where humans may fail, technology gives us a way to create the perfect "Frankenstein take." This can apply to any instrument or vocal recording if you take the time to edit it properly.

Noise Reduction

If you are recording in a home studio, you must be the luckiest person on Earth to be able to bypass noise reduction in the editing process. Even in a professional studio, there are going to be moments of dead air that need to come out, the shuffling of the vocalist's feet or people walking in the studio. There are lots of normal sounds that come with the presence of a human in a room. If you have sensitive microphones, they could even pick up the sound of the vocalist breathing or someone chatting or coughing. You might catch sounds coming off the amps.

To do this, the inactive spaces between recordings of instruments or vocals are cut from the track. If there is some background noise that leaks into the recording, a high-pass filter could fix the issue by running it over the lower-end of the frequency. The important thing here is to make sure that you're only using this on non-bass recordings.

Pitch Editing

Pitch editing is primarily used to adjust pitchy vocals, bringing an off-note back to a pleasant listening experience. However, this does not mean it cannot have a positive effect on the instrumentals that build your melodies. Auto-Tune is a popular software used to adjust these off-key moments in the recording, but there are all kinds that you can test, depending on your preferred sound.

Time Editing

Where pitch editing clears up the vocal pitch, time editing adjusts tempo issues in instrumentation. When something in a track sounds off-beat, but it's otherwise a good recording, you can adjust the timing of the song using one of two ways:

• Time stretching involves running the piece of off-beat music through a plug-in to adjust the tempo of the track so that it matches the rest of the song. This works with almost all instruments.

- The cut and paste method is a little more hands-on. It's exactly what it sounds like, cutting and pasting pieces of the off-beat section to fall in line with the song's tempo. This is particularly effective when dealing with percussion.

CHAPTER 7

ALL ABOUT MIXING

———————◆○◆———————

Mixing is the process of making your collection of soundtracks *sound like a song*. When you're first starting, it's easy to just look at mixing as the time to add effects to your instrumentals and vocals. While technically, yes, that *is* a part of it, there's so much more to the mixing process. Mixing makes the individual pieces of the song more cohesive and blends them into the base template that will later become the fully mastered track. By the time you're done mixing, each track of recorded material will be virtually perfected and ready to be blended into your final product.

Prep

When it comes time to get into the brunt of the work and dig into the mixing process, it will benefit you to no end to have your workspace organized and ready to go. Preparing and organizing your DAW session can make the work go faster, and frankly, more enjoyable. There are twelve core steps to organizing your DAW that will uncomplicate your life, broken down into an accessible checklist.

- *Organize all tracks by instrument.* Ideally, you have a system that you can rely on consistently, so I recommend organizing them in a way that you can easily replicate on future tracks. Muscle memory is a great tool in this kind of work. It also helps to keep like-things together. For example, keep all of your percussion instruments grouped together, your strings together, your vocals together, etc. There is nothing more frustrating than trying to remember where you left your snare when it is trapped between your vocals and your keyboard. Make it make as much sense as possible.

- *Get rid of useless tracks.* Once you've done your import on all your recorded tracks, give them each a listen. If something is just dead air, or if you really can't see yourself using something, whether it's poor quality or it does not fit your vision for the song, get rid of it. It's taking up space for nothing, and you only want to keep viable tracks within reach. This leads me to my next point:

- *If you're not sure about a track, hide it.* This will keep it in the session, and it'll be easy to access if you think you might have a use for it after all. These tracks are hidden gems just as often as they go unused, so if you're uncertain, just hide it so that it's still on hand instead of deleting it.

- *Rename your file to something easily recognized.* "17_audio_09232021" isn't super specific and is going to make it complicated to find your tracks. It helps to name them based on the section of the song, instrument, and any other significant identifying information. Keep it concise, but clear.

- *Color code for easy identification.* Again, if you can establish a color-coding system that you'll replicate on future mixes, you'll make your life easier by allowing yourself to build that muscle memory. For example, I tend to keep my percussion in shades of red, vocals in shades of purple, strings in shades of blue, and electronic material in shades of orange and yellow. Additional samples and sound bites that I might use go into shades of green, and so on. Build a system and trust the system.

- *Set all like instruments into buses.* If you are unfamiliar with bussing, think of it this way: a school bus picks up similar people, the students, all going to the same place, the school. In this scenario, if you have three different sections of drums, and each is recorded using six microphones, you are looking at having *eighteen* different tracks for drums. Putting all those tracks together on a bus means that they all land under a single master fader. Now, instead of having to put each track through a compressor, a single pass with a compressor will handle all eighteen tracks at once.

- *Add in your crossfades and fades.* A crossfade helps to join two pieces of audio smoothly, instead of there being an abrupt change in sound when one ends and the other begins. Most DAWs available these days have a function to add space for crossfades to the entire session, both at the beginning and end of each track. about ten ms at both ends of the track is enough to allow for smooth transitioning.

- *Go through your files to gain staging.* The goal of gain staging is to bring the volume of each track to the holy grail of volume, called the "Sweet Spot" since the 1960s; that sweet level of 0 dBVU. This means that your track is not going to be too busy and noisy at some points, and too dull and faded at others. We will go over the individual steps of gain staging after this checklist, but at this point, the most important information to remember is that if the gain of a channel peaks over -6 dBFS, the gain needs to be reduced. If a channel peaks below -30 dBFS, bring the gain up.

- *Input both the time signatures and tempo data.* This information will be necessary to make your life easier when it comes time for automation and editing. Don't skip this information just to save time. It will become crucial later.

- *Create labels for each section of your song.* Having your verses, your chorus, and any other sections in use labeled for quick access is invaluable, as both a time and sanity saver.

- *Bring your buffering size way up.* If your buffering size is high, it will reduce your CPU usage. Ideally, your buffer size should be set to about 1024.

- *Find and import similar reference tracks.* This means going through songs that have been professionally produced, mixed, and mastered, and finding the songs that have similar qualities to the song you're looking to create, as well as songs that inspire you and have details that you'd like to replicate. Having something to reference keeps your work in perspective. We all think we have incredible memories that we can work from, but the reality is that there is *a lot* going on throughout the mixing and mastering. Reliably working from memory isn't something that can be done unless you are a musical genius of unmatched reputation. Most of us, unfortunately, are not these incredible geniuses.

Further Information on Gain Staging

Gain staging doesn't have to be daunting. Six steps with a gain staging plug-in are all that stand between you and the golden *sweet spot.*

1. Whichever your preferred gain staging plug-in is, load it up at the top of any tracks that peak higher than -6dBFS.

2. Good gain plug-ins should come with a VU meter. Set it to the beginning of your stereo output. The VU meter should then be calibrated to -18dBFS.

3. Go through each track and solo them. Play the tracks at the loudest point.

4. While the track is playing at its loudest point, adjust the gain lower until you see on the VU meter that the needle is mainly holding at the analog sweet spot: 0 dB. Yes, you're going to have to do this for each track.

5. Once you have gone through each track, repeat the process on the instrument bus you've gotten through the tracks of the bus. This is to ensure consistency overall.

6. After working through each track and bus, repeat steps 1-5 on tracks that are peaking below -30dBFS so that

you can raise the gain, bringing the tracks, and then subsequently, the instrument busses up to -0 dB.

Volume Balance

Volume is a big deal when it comes to music production; the louder you're listening to your track, the better it sounds. While volume can make a flawed song sound good, bringing the volume down can highlight sound quality issues, or bring out the smaller flaws that make the song sound awful when played at lower volumes. Our goal is to keep a consistent quality for the song, regardless of the volume it's played at. While working with the volume balance, your monitors should be set to conversation volume; this is to say, the volume should be loud enough to hear and work on, but if you were to have a friend or colleague in the room with you, you could still easily have a conversation with them.

After you have wrapped up your prep work for mixing, the next thing that you must nail down is your volume balance. When recording, different pieces may be collected at different volumes. Getting a consistent volume will help your mix sound like it is ready for publishing and will make it easier to hear the changes you make, or where changes still need to be made.

Setting up your volume balance starts with double-checking your gain peaking. After gaining staging during the preparation stage, your tracks *should* be leveled without any major peaking. Before you start the work on volume balancing, make sure that there are no tracks that are peaking too much; if they are, adjust the gain so that the gain is consistent.

Once the gain is consistent, find the loudest part of your song. Set this part on a loop, then bring all of your faders way down. Flip to your reference tracks and give them a listen for their volume levels. You will want to regularly flip back and forth between your mixing and your references to keep you on track. Listen for what you hear prioritized in the song, then look at the pieces of your song for what you feel should be prioritized first. For example, vocals are often a top priority. Whichever is your most important channel, bring it up to -5dB. From there, bring your second most important channel up, and balance it with your first channel. Keep doing this until you have your volume balanced through all your recorded channels.

Take a break from the song and walk away to let your ears rest. It is ideal that after doing balancing work you can come back to the project with fresh ears. Usually, on the first listen through the song after taking a quick break, it is easy to pick up what needs to be adjusted to bring the track to balance. Once you have made your post-break adjustments, play the entire song through, and tweak your instruments as needed. Make sure to give the full song a listen at a high volume *and* low volume before moving on to the next stage.

Compression

Compression is used throughout mixing and mastering and is an important tool to understand well. This process compresses noise down, bringing everything out to the same level, and sometimes removing small noises altogether. There are seven key components of a compressor that you should understand before compressing your tracks.

Attack Time is how quickly the compression will engage when the gain reaches the set limit and begins reducing the audio. Typically, it is best to have a slower attack time to build up the excitement of the song. A faster attack time can make an instrument sound controlled, with more body to the sound.

The **Gain Reduction Meter** shows you how hard the compressor is working by tracking just how much gain is being reduced during compression.

Knee controls how obvious the compression is. A hard knee (0.0) keeps the compression obvious, versus a soft knee (1.0) that blends the sound of the compression into the track.

Makeup Gain brings back some of the volume lost during the compression process since compression reduces the volume of the track it is being used on.

Ratio applies to how aggressively the volume is reduced through compression. Higher ratios mean a heavier compression on sound and volume. When reading ratio, flip the numbers; if your ratio is 2:1, the volume will be reduced by half a decibel, if it is 4:1, then it is reduced by a quarter decibel, etc.

Release Time refers to how many milliseconds it takes for the compressor to completely disengage from compression and return to the normal levels.

Threshold is how the compressor knows when to kick in. The threshold limit is set to the point of gain reduction that the track needs. Once the gain reaches the set threshold, compression turns on, releasing when the gain drops below the threshold level. The lower the threshold is set, the more compression is used in the track.

The following checklist is a good place to start your experimentation with compression. It's important to note that compression depends on genre as much as anything else. Some genres barely touch compression, such as genres that heavily rely on instrumental representation, whereas genres that focus more on vocals, such as pop, rock, country, or rap, will use more compression. This is where practicing and training your ear makes all the difference in the quality of the mixing in your tracks.

- *Adjust your ratio to 3:1 to start.*

- *Adjust your threshold so that you're getting about 10dBs of gain reduction.*

- *Set your attack time low, to about 100 ms to start.*

- *Now set your release time fast, to about 5 ms.*

- *Go back to the attack time. Decrease the attack time until the transient sounds are dull and flat, then pull back a bit so that it's just outside that sound quality.*

- *Increase the release knob until your compressor seems to breathe with the song. When you look at kick and snare; the gain reduction meter should hit zero between each hit.*

- *Return to the threshold knob and increase it until you get your preferred level of dynamic control, sound thickness, and aggression in the music. This typically comes out to about 1-2dBs of gain reduction.*

- *Return to your ratio knob. This is where you can adjust the compression to your personal taste. If you want subtlety in your compression, bring the ratio to about 2:1. If you want something more aggressive, go up to around 4:1.*

- *Adjust makeup gain so that you can accommodate for any volume that was lost during the compression process.*

EQ (Equalization)

An equalizer shapes the tones within the frequencies of your track to create a cohesive, professional track. The frequency spectrum is measured in hertz or Hz in shorthand. This covers the full spectrum of human hearing; lower notes, like bass, will be heard in the lower ranges of Hertz, typically around 50 Hz. A higher note will register higher on the spectrum, such as 3000 Hz, or 3 kHz.

On EQ plug-ins, you will typically see the frequency range from 20 Hz up to 20 kHz, which covers the full range of human hearing. These frequencies can be broken down into five sections that you will work with during the equalization process.

Sub-Bass (20-60 Hz)

If you have ever been in a nightclub and felt that deep rumbling in your chest as the bass thumps through the room, that's the sub-bass. Typically, the sub-bass is not something you hear a lot of. You might catch it if you're listening to a song with a really good subwoofer or a quality set of open-back headphones, but in general, the sub-bass is more easily felt than it is heard. Anything under 60 Hz is considered sub-bass.

Bass (60-200 Hz)

Bass builds the foundation of your songs, along with the percussive instruments. You'll get bass from a bass guitar, or sometimes in vocals. This range of frequency is easily heard and could be described as a deep rumbling sound. If you leave the bass out of your mix, chances are the track will sound like there's a piece missing, leaving the track too open.

Low-Mids (200-600 Hz)

Low-mids are great, but they can be a problem area if there is too much in the song; they can make your sound muddy, which can be a pain once you reach mixing and mastering. Low-mids come from the top end of bass guitar, certain ranges of vocals, and in the lower building ranges of guitar and other instruments.

Mids (600 Hz - 3 kHz)

The mids are where most of our range of hearing sits, so this range is incredibly important to get right. This is where you should be focusing on giving your vocals full attention, and melodies should come into full focus. However, tread carefully, because going overboard can bring in harshness and aggression that can become overwhelming.

Upper-Mids (3-8 kHz)

Especially when dealing with vocals, this range can be tricky. When done right, it can offer a song a range of clarity. Otherwise, this range becomes brittle and harsh, ruining this end of the listening experience.

Highs (8-20 kHz)

Everything above 8 kHz is considered the high-end of the spectrum. Between 8-12 kHz is typically what we would consider treble. 12 kHz and above is what we would consider air.

Putting EQ to Work

Where volume has faders to move the loudness up and down, EQ does the same thing for frequency waves in order to alter the tone of a sound. If something is sounding too bright, it can be shifted into the right place, or boosted until it sounds its absolute best. There are seven tools and terms you need to understand in order to do this to the best of your ability.

Bell filtering centers around a single frequency. You should get to know this filter well, as it is one of the most commonly used in EQ.

Frequency tells you which area of the spectrum that you are currently working with and indicates how far you are making adjustments. This is good to bear in mind, so you know which area of frequency you may be moving into.

High Pass Filter (HPF) cuts the lower end of the frequency so that the upper end can be singled out and adjusted accordingly, without having to try to listen through bass. This can bring out areas that need a word that would not be so obvious while still hearing the lower end.

Low Pass Filter (LPF) cuts the high-end, letting you focus on the lower-end to decipher areas that can be adjusted.

Q ranges between 0.0 and 1.0, and lets you know how wide your filter is. The lower the number is, the wider your filter is.

Shelf filters flatten the frequency, on either end of the spectrum that you happen to need. This flattening can cut or boost the frequency as needed.

Spectrum is the full range of sound that we can hear, going from 20 Hz to 20 kHz.

The filters of the EQ are used to cut and boost different areas of the spectrum to be manipulated accordingly. This leaves you to wonder what areas to affect to use them effectively. There are four core problems that the EQ process makes quick work of, once you've spent time manipulating the filters.

- EQ allows you to carve out space in the mix. If certain instruments are crowding your vocals, cutting them back can make room for the vocals to shine through. Even just a few kHz can make a difference.

- Wide cuts and boosts can enhance the sounds that are doing good things for your mix. An EQ sweep can help you find the parts that sound the best or the parts that are too overpowering but could still work. Start by bringing these areas up or down by 3 dB, and then adjust it until it suits your taste.

- The filters can also completely alter the sound in a new way. This can introduce new effects to the sound before you even get into the effects portion of mixing.

- Aside from enhancing, doing an EQ sweep can also help you locate portions that can be taken out. A narrow cut can help to remove room resonance. Go in with a bell filter, boosted all the way with the Q sitting at about 1.5, then slowly move it left and right until you find an area that is too loud or just plain sounds bad, and cut it. A high pass filter can also cut noise from the lower end but should be used sparingly.

It's key to have an idea of what you want to hear happen as you're going into the EQ stage of mixing. While it can be a good idea to fiddle with these things when you're first starting out and acclimating your ear to the effects of these filters, as you get to the point of comfort with the tools at your disposal you should have an idea or plan on what you hope to accomplish. The "fiddling stage" shouldn't carry on too heavily once you have a good handle on your DAW.

Space (Panning, Reverb, and Delay)

At this stage of your mixing process, your sound is very much one-dimensional. When you're getting ready to work the spacing of the track, it helps to imagine it as being performed on a stage. Right now, the one-dimensionality of the track is like lining up every instrument to be played elbow to elbow on the stage in a tiny cluster. Music needs *space* to thrive. The music needs space to open and gain dimension.

Delay

Delay is a precise method of creating an echo effect. It's an exact repetition of a sound and is a fantastic way to push vocals to the front and center point of attention. Delay creates space around vocals and instruments without risking drowning anything out or pushing them back into the background.

Creating Delay Around Vocals

1. Create an aux track that you will send your vocals to for adding stereo delay.

2. Set your delay to 100% wet, and then unlink left and right channels. One side should be set to 20-50 ms and the other set to 50-200 ms. Bear in mind that the longer the delay, the more obvious it will be when listening back. When there is more space between the two channels, it'll give your vocals a wider sound.

3. Test your feedback between 0-15%, depending on how natural you want to keep your sound.

4. Set an EQ just before the Stereo Delay. Choose a low filter and work it up slowly until the sound starts to seem thin. Try to avoid cutting more than 300 Hz. Then choose a high filter and work it down until the delay starts getting lost in the vocals. Avoid cutting any lower than 3 kHz.

5. Finally, adjust the volume. Turn the aux track volume down, give your ears a minute to acclimate, and then steadily turn it up until it sounds good. Then, just for good measure, bring it down a few decibels.

If you are hoping to add delay to your melodic instruments, stereo slapback delay works fantastically to broaden the sound and give the instrument more depth.

Panning

If you've ever had any exposure to ASMR, you know panning well, even if you didn't know the name. Panning is the shifting of the sound, making the sound of the voice or instrument seem as though it's moving from left to right. If you go back to imagining that your instruments are elbow-to-elbow to each other on a stage, panning is what gives a second dimension to the sound and takes the instruments from being clustered together at the front of the stage, to have their own space on either side of the stage.

This is probably one of the simplest parts of mixing; the panning knob is typically located right on the channel strip. Move the knob to the left or right, depending on where you want the sound to move. There are a handful of optimal placements; 100% to the left or right, 50% to the left or right, and centered. The very last thing on the topic of panning is that melodies and low-end instruments should not be panned to either side. They make the most of their impact when centered. Vocals can benefit from small amounts of panning for effect but do not overdo it or it becomes too much.

Reverb

If panning spaces the band out on the stage from left to right, and the delay adds dimension to the sound, reverb is how you place the instruments at varying distances from front to back. This is how we introduce depth.

If you are recording in a perfectly sound-treated room, sometimes the recording can sound flat. With reverb, you reintroduce the sounds of a room perfectly. It can also create some distance between the instrument and the listener. There are two ways we do this; creating a room and changing the tone.

Creating a Room

1. Start with creating two aux tracks. One should be labeled "Room Tone," the other labeled "Ambiance." Each should have a reverb plug-in placed onto it.

2. Next comes setting up the room. For your room tone track, the balance should be set to 100% wet, with late

reflections. Decay is best when set between 500-3000 ms, and pre-delay set to 0-75 ms. The distance can range between 15-50%.

3. The ambiance uses the same balance, 100% wet, but with early reflections. The decay should be set to 250-750 ms, with pre-delay set to 2-25 ms. Distance should fall between 1-5%.

4. This is where you bring your instruments into the aux tracks. You will be sending a bit of each instrument to both tracks. Sending the instrument back in space means putting more of it into Ambiance. To keep it front and center, but more of the track in room tone.

5. Put an EQ on before the reverb. Move a high pass filter up until the track starts thinning. If the mix begins to sound too dark, a shelf boost to brighten it up. If it's too bright, a shelf cut is how you'll want to turn down the bright sound. If you find the sound is becoming muddy, go to your low-mids, and cut between 3-10dBs.

6. Finally, adjust your volume. Start by bringing it all the way down, then slowly bring the volume knobs back up until it's at an enjoyable, pleasant level. Then, for the sake of safety, bring it back down by 1-3dBs.

Volume Automation

Up until this point, you have been looping the loudest section of the song. While the work you have put in on this section of the song likely sounds amazing, playing through the whole song might sound a little bit off; the volume on the rest of the song won't match what you have done up to this point. Luckily, it won't be difficult to match the volume on the rest of the work. Automation allows us to match the volume we just set on the loudest section of our song to the rest of the song to give us a cohesive, level sound.

Begin by opening your automation channel. You will want to create points around the sections where you want to bring the volume up and pull it up. If you want to create a more natural listening experience, your volume should slope at the beginning and end of the song, building up in the beginning, and sloping back down at the end as the song fades.

Volume automation also has the benefit of adding excitement and maintaining listener engagement. Shifting the volume on some instruments up by a decibel or two right before a chorus can bring a big burst of energy to the song. We also know that when the vocals pause in a song, people tend to lose some interest. Bringing the volume up by a decibel or so while waiting for the vocals to come back in can retain that interest and hype while listening.

Effects

Alright, so by now you have gotten rid of the useless tracks, you have arranged your instruments on the virtual stage, everything is equalized and compressed into perfection, and your volume is perfect across the board. Now, you get to dive into the fun part that everyone thinks of when they think of the mixing stage, adding in effects. This is where you get to *play*.

The range of effects available online is endless and they cover a wide range of possibilities. You can download many types of software and plug-ins that can do all manner of things and create millions of sounds. These are both paid and free to download. I encourage you to embrace your creativity and experiment with all kinds of effects that suit your style and preference. Of course, do not overdo it or you will end up with a busy and overwhelming track.

Final Checks

The final check is about tweaking things before your mix goes into the mastering process. Go through every last detail, take your time, and tweak whatever you feel could use the adjustment. Just bear in mind that when you change one tool, it can change the effects of other tools. Compression will lower the volume and distortion may create harshness.

As you've had to do several times through this process, give yourself at least a 12-hour break between finishing mixing and doing your final sweep through the song. Let your ears rest, then come back with fresh ears and minds. Listen to the song from beginning to end in a variety of spaces, and take notes on anything that feels off, and should be taken care of before you start the mastering process.

My final note on the final sweep is to remember that you have reference tracks for a reason! Use them to make sure that your track sounds comparable to a professionally released track. When you take the time to listen to your reference tracks, you're more likely to catch the areas in your own track that does not sound as great, or that can be improved.

CHAPTER 8

MASTERING YOUR TRACK

———————◆◇◆———————

Mastering is the final step in the magic journey of producing a track. By the end of mastering, you have your final product in a single, refiled file, ready to be sent out for distribution and promotion whenever you like. Some people perceive mastering as about making a track louder. *Technically*, they aren't wrong; a part of the mastering process does make the track easy to perceive as louder. The mastering process also makes the track more translatable for different devices and environments, as well as improves the overall quality of the song better.

Creating a mastered track also helps when putting together an EP or LP album. Each of the tracks will be played at the same volume and in the same tone, offering a consistent listening experience. Mastering should bring the track up to the same sound quality as what is played on the radio and streaming services.

The mastering of a track is typically one step where you pass the track off to a mastering engineer. There are two reasons for this: one, they have studied this topic extensively, it is what they focus on. They can bring the track up in quality in ways that the rest of us mere onlookers could not imagine. Two, they offer a second set of ears that can be unbiased. When we have spent hours, days, or weeks on a project, between writing it, recording it, and then editing it, we become deaf to the poorer qualities of the song. Some parts begin to sound normal to us which brings down the overall quality of the song, or just plain sounds *bad*. They can be more objective about the quality of the track, coming in with fresh ears.

If time is a factor, you can also use mastering software that runs the song through an algorithm. The algorithm adjusts the song so that it sounds more like a radio quality song, but given that it's an algorithm, it isn't perfect. If you are hoping for a quick clean-up, they're a great option, but I don't recommend relying on them heavily if you can avoid it. They can offer a solid base of adjustments for you to then adjust yourself until the track is perfected and ready for publishing. Of course, if finances are a factor in your decision, or if you just prefer to handle the whole process yourself, there are lots of ways that you can increase your skills in mastering.

I will suggest that you take some time away from the project, just to give yourself some time to gain some objectivity when listening back to it before you start mastering. Work on other songs and get the song out of your head for a little while before you come back to get started.

Prep Work

The biggest portion of mastering a track is found in *preparing* to master the track.

Begin by double-checking your acoustic treatment and placement of your studio monitors. Mastering needs to happen in a sound optimized environment. Otherwise, sounds and imperfections can be easily missed. A key component to the mastering process is making sure that the track sounds amazing no matter how it is played, so mastering in a proper sound-treated environment is important to ensure that your track will sound incredible no matter how good or bad a person's headphones or speakers are, or where they happen to be listening.

If there is a reason that prevents you from being able to do your mastering in a sound-treated space, a good pair of headphones is the next best option.

Make sure you're done mixing. Go over the pieces of your track one final time and ensure that you have everything done. Give each section another listen and check for flaws in all areas, and that everything sounds as close to what you want to hear in your final product as you can get it. Take the time to go over your saturation and panning to give your mix body, and excitement, and ensure a stereo quality mix before reaching the official mastering. Mastering can't start until your mix is completed, but that doesn't mean that you should not reach for it sounds like it has been mastered already. Anything you can do to minimize the work done in mastering will be a benefit in the end.

Go over your levels. This is to make sure that you're not getting any clipping from the faders. Take your time to find any kinds of distortion in each track; it's easy to miss clipping and other issues while mixing, especially while working multiple sections at a time. If these imperfections find their way into the mastering process, they become glaring neon signs pointing to what's gone wrong in the mixing.

While looking over *all* of the faders, none of them should be in red. Each fader should have a good amount of headroom, with the decibel points peaking between -4 and -6 dB.

Bounce your track. All this means is taking all the pieces of your track and turning them into a single file. Consistency isn't just recommended, it's necessary. If the recording was done at 48 kHz resolution, it should be bounced down at the same resolution, just like the bit rate should remain the same. The file type you bounce down to should *always* be exported as a .aiff or .wav file, and not an MP3 file. This comes at the end of the mastering process. It is important to note that, should you be using DAW at this point in the process, to make sure that you don't use the normalize feature. It'll only make the track louder, and not in a good way. This will be dealt with later in the mastering process, so hold back, and trust the process.

Walk away from the project. Take at least a day away from the project to reset your ears and let you regain objectivity. Work on another project, take a minimum of a day to focus on something other than the mixing and mastering of the track, or anything that will give you time to get the song out of your head and ears. Preferably, you should take a few days to move on to other music, but even a week or more is ideal. Give yourself ample amounts of space from the song to come back to it with the freshest ears you can on the schedule you have available.

Start the next project and import any references. I cannot stress the value of using references during your mastering process. While mastering in a vacuum, you could be making decisions that sound great in a sound-treated environment but sound like garbage when compared to work that has been published and played on radios all over the world. Choose songs that carry the same energy as what you are hoping to produce and compare them regularly to the track you're currently working up.

When importing the reference files, import them onto different tracks beneath the file you plan on mastering. This will help to prevent you from mixing anything up and make them easy to access, rather than bouncing between apps or software. Hearing it through the same program that you're working on will give you more information to compare and simplify the overall process.

Grab your pen and paper, listen to the track, and take notes. This should be your first time listening to the track since completing the mixing and beginning your mastering prep work. Pay attention; any detail that seems even vaguely off, or like it isn't top quality, make a note of it. Make note of the point in the song and the issue you're noticing, even if you think it might be insignificant. If it sounds off to you, it'll be even more obvious to someone who is hearing the song for the very first time, since they never had the opportunity to hear the error or weirdness grow into its position in the current track.

The most important thing is to set aside your ego and pride and be entirely honest and realistic with yourself on this first listen. The vast majority of the errors and issues will jump out at you within the first listen. The very first time listening to the song is one of the most important points in the mastering process when your ears are at their freshest and you've had time to separate yourself from the track. Be honest and humble with yourself, and you'll have no problem with making your list of problem areas. This list will become the key to your mastering process as you work through each section to correct the flaws and create a beautifully mastered piece.

Listen to your song *everywhere*. While you're still in your studio setting, go back and forth between listening to your reference songs, and listening to your song. Take notes on the key differences; what is too much, where is the song lacking, and what simply doesn't compare at all. Once you've had a few listens, take the track on tour. Listen to it in different rooms of your home and compare it to your references once again. Make your notes, no matter how insignificant you perceive them to be. Listen using different types and qualities of headphones, listen to it on a speaker in your backyard, through your television and consumer quality stereo speakers. Bring the track into your car, and if you are so lucky, see if you can get yourself into a venue that might allow a few minutes during off-hours to check out how your track sounds compared to your references. Listening in as many different places, devices, and situations to give you a more well-rounded idea of where your song needs to improve to reach popular media on the radio levels of sound quality and success. While listening, make sure that the volume is the same between you and the reference files you're using; otherwise, it may trick your mind into thinking that there are more problems than there are.

Depending on the software you are using, you should also take a look at the sound wave charts. If your frequencies are all over the place in comparison to your reference tracks, then you know you have work to put in still. Bear in mind that these songs are different, the charts will always be different at this step, but glaring issues will make themselves visible to you. Note the volume that the tracks are playing at, both yours and the reference tracks you are using. If the volume of the tracks is all over the place, you will lack consistency in your comparison, and miss all kinds of little details that can make or break the sound of your finished mastered track. A VU meter plug-in is a great way to double-check what needs to be balanced in the volume of your reference tracks compared to your own. As you get more accustomed to this part of the process, you'll be able to rely more on doing it by ear, but it never hurts to run it through the software to verify if you are not sure.

Before you get into the meat of your mastering, you should also put your song through a low-end pass filter. This is particularly helpful for those who are unfamiliar with the mastering process. This will help you figure out if the lower-end of your song is too loud or if it is lacking in energy. From there, once you've compared your songs, you can go straight to the levels of the lower-end mix and adjust them accordingly. If you find that the bass or the lower-end of your kicks is getting lost, instead of cranking up the levels, bring up the mid to help the sound come through. Even the difference of 1 kHz can completely alter the way your low-end comes through. Once you have adjusted your levels, if you want to double-check that you're on par with your reference, run the VU or RMS meter again, but this time, with the low-end pass filter on. This can give you a visual aid to make sure you have not gone too far in either direction.

Working on Your Master Track

Adjust your dynamics using compression. We will be working with six knobs in setting this compression: the ratio, attack, threshold, knee, release, and makeup gain. When compressing your whole track overall, it is important to know that a little bit can take you the distance. At the absolute most, 3dBs is *plenty* of gain reduction. Typically, you'll want to aim for 1-2dBs, without surpassing 3dBs.

The process of adjusting your dynamics can be broken down into the same nine-step checklist as doing general compression during mixing:

- *Adjust your ratio to 3:1 to start.*

- *Adjust your threshold so that you are getting about 10dBs of gain reduction.*

- *Set your attack time low to about 100 ms to start.*

- *Now set your release time fast, to about 5 ms.*

- *Go back to the attack time. Decrease the attack time until the transient sounds are dull and flat, then pull back a bit so that it is just outside that sound quality.*

- *Increase the release knob until your compressor seems to breathe with the song. When you look at kick and snare, the gain reduction meter should hit zero between each hit.*

- *Return to the threshold knob and increase it until you get your preferred level of dynamic control, sound thickness, and aggression in the music. This typically comes out to about 1-2dBs of gain reduction.*

- *Return to your ratio knob. This is where you can adjust the compression to your taste. If you want subtlety in your compression, bring the ratio to about*

2:1. If you want something more aggressive, go up to around 4:1.

- *Adjust makeup gain so that you can accommodate for any volume lost during the compression process.*

These nine steps should lead to optimal compression. The key is to make sure there are modest shifts in the knobs because on the overall track, the slightest changes can make the most dramatic differences. Unlike during mixing, you'll rarely want to be cranking knobs in any direction. Some things should be noted about the compression process.

- If you have an auto-release function, use it to your advantage. This will provide a more natural sound to your track. If you do not have an auto-release function, try your release around 150 ms, and adjust from there.

- Do not rely on visuals if you do not have to. *Listen* to your track. A visual, like VU meters, will help you in the beginning while you are figuring things out in the mastering process, but training your ears to recognize if your song is sounding flat or too busy will give you an advantage when you are going into your mixing process for your next song.

- When dealing with attack time, move slowly. If your attack time is too fast, the song goes flat. Too slow, and it becomes far too aggressive. Try starting it around 10 ms; if you're working on a slower song, bring it down a little at a time. For a faster song, tweak it upwards a little.

Fixing tone using EQ and multiband compression. This is the point where you're going to go back to the notes you made during your first listen-through, as well as while listening in multiple environments. During this process, you'll adjust where your track sounds too muddy, or where your high or low-end is too much or too little.

During mastering, a linear EQ is going to be your best friend. It affects a multitude of instruments all at once and can help to make your track sound clean. Where you may have been using narrow cuts and boosts during the mixing process, now you want to turn to wide cuts and boosts. Just as with the compression, your changes should be subtle, at most boosting or cutting about 3dBs. Following this, if you find there's too much boom, or that the bass or low-end of your song is still too prominent, using a little bit of a high-pass filter can help reduce that booming, overly bassy sound.

Multiband compression is used when you feel that there are parts of the song that are inconsistent with the rest. This is specifically for areas of the song that you find may have too much bass, or where the high-end is coming out too strong. Trying to adjust these things without a multiband compressor will affect the whole song; this isn't what you want.

When adjusting the inconsistencies of the song, use your multiband compressor to select the frequencies you're hoping to work on and go about the same way you would with regular compression. It's all the same functions and knobs, just on very specific sections of the song. Multiband compression does come with a few differences though.

If you're using it to quiet a section of a song, keep in mind not to overdo it; up to 3dBs is plenty. Compression will also make that section quieter naturally, so avoid using the makeup gain. You will work against your goal if you are using the makeup gain at this point by turning the softer sounds in the song up, causing another level of imbalance. You should also avoid using multiple bands if you can because this can complicate the entire process and make errors even more likely. Multiband compression isn't necessary for every song, so only use it when you need it.

Adding enhancements. This step isn't always necessary. If your track doesn't need any kind of enhancement, you can skip this step altogether. There are three types of enhancements that you can add at this time: volume automation, saturation, and stereo widening.

Stereo widening helps to spread out the sounds within the song to give it a larger sound. This should be used sparingly, and only when necessary. When played in mono instead of stereo, stereo widening can make the song sound significantly worse, introducing all kinds of phasing issues. If you do not need it, skip over this option.

Saturation adds color to your mix, filling it out when your song is sounding flat or thin. Be careful with overusing saturation; if you're using it where it isn't needed, or using it at excessively high levels, you can create distortion. Oversaturation can lead to an even flatter, distorted sound, which ruins the mix overall.

Volume automation makes slight adjustments to the volume. For example, you might use it to slightly raise or lower the decibel level going into the chorus or verse. Be careful that you don't go above or below a decibel or so and pay attention to the sloping of the sound. Without sloping, the sound change will not only be noticeable, but harsh and abrupt to the listener. Volume automation should be used to make an impact, but not to the degree that it seems like the chorus is suddenly kicking you in the teeth.

Limit the track. Remember how we said we would make the song perceivably louder through mastering? This is where we bring the loudness of the song up to the others in the genre. Limiting makes sure you don't have a quiet, dull track after all the work you've put in. A limiter is like a regular compressor, but instead of a 2:1 or 3:1 ratio, we work with the "brick wall" ratio: ∞:1. This means that absolutely no sound within the song will exceed the set limit.

- *Set your output ceiling.* When setting the limit on a song, we typically aim for around 0dBs. When setting the ceiling, you want to give it a little room, between 0.3dB and 0.8dB. This will ensure that your track doesn't cut when played through speakers with gain boosting built-in.

- *Increase your input gain so that you are getting about 10dBs gain reduction.*

- *Adjust the attack to 100 ms so that it slows down.*

- *Slow down your release to about 500 ms.*

- *Go back to your attack and decrease it.* Do this until you start to hear the track distorting and losing the impact, then back up to the point before the distortion begins.

- *Go back to the release and decrease it.* Do as you did with the attack. Decrease until the track begins to distort, then back off to the point just before the distortion begins. If your compressor has an auto function for this, feel free to use it. This will provide a natural sound.

- *Decrease input gain.* As per the general rule of this process, stay within 1-3dBs of gain reduction.

Final checks. At this point, you are in reach of a completed track. Take time away from your track, even if it is only a few hours or a night to sleep on it. Go over the details of the track one final time. Make sure that your dynamics are where they need to be, compare the track to your reference tracks, and check all of your levels. This is like the Carpenter's axiom: measure twice, cut once. In this case, listen twice, bounce out once. You can run your track through dynamic and level checkers to ensure that the sound quality compares to professionally mastered and released tracks.

Bounce out. Bouncing means exporting the file to a format that can be used by different playback systems. You are going to bounce it into two types of files, one in MP3 and the other in a lossless file type, such as .caf, .aiff, or .wav. When you bounce your track, check your resolution. Audio tracks are bounced in 16 bits, and a sample rate of 44.1 kHz. Do not forget to dither your track. Most DAW programs automatically do this. This means ensuring that there isn't any distortion that finds its way into the track during bouncing. If your DAW automatically dithers the track, the selection POW-r 2 is one of the best to use for most tracks. Never dither a track more than once, or you may potentially create noise and distortion in your track. Finally, if your DAW has a normalized function, make sure it is turned OFF. Normalizing is not going to be any good at this stage. Normalizing is used to make the song louder and given that you have spent all this time mastering, the crudeness of the normalized function won't add anything of value to your track.

CHAPTER 9

THE MUSIC BUSINESS

———◆◇◆———

The music industry involves much more than creating an amazing track or being a talented vocalist or musician. It is called a business for a reason: a level of business savvy is necessary to get yourself going and make a decent income from doing what you love. Some might look at it as a 50/50 endeavor; if you put three days into developing your skills, then you should put three days into the business side as well.

Music Lawyers: Do You Need One?

While there are some areas of the music business that are straightforward to figure out if you are willing to take the time to educate yourself, there are some points where you might benefit from a music lawyer. This is going to vary depending on the group, artist, and legal experience of everyone involved. If you are savvy in legal jargon, then perhaps you might be fine to move forward, but otherwise, it may help to have a music lawyer on retainer to make sure that all paperwork is sound and fair for all parties.

Contracts

A music lawyer is ideal for explaining what is happening within a contract and helping you decide if the set contract is fair for all parties. A music lawyer can also figure out where there is room for negotiation and can keep you from signing something that will be detrimental to your work, income, and wellbeing. Contracts could be coming from a label, or they could be used to establish percentages between yourself and other partners and service providers. This can include royalties, as well as organizing split sheets. Split sheets establish the percentages from each song going to each person, depending on the work they contributed to the song. If you wrote the song, the lyrics, recorded most of the song, and just had a drummer come in to do their part, it makes sense that you aren't going to split royalties 50/50. A music lawyer can make sure that everything is in order and fair according to contribution.

Copyright Laws

When it comes time to either copyright your music, or if you are not sure how to navigate doing covers, a music lawyer can guide you through what you need to know. You don't necessarily need a music lawyer to copyright every song, but they can make sure you know what you're doing and what to look for to prevent you from being handed a lawsuit.

Legal Advice

In general, if you're concerned with the legality of something, or if someone is attempting to take advantage of you, but you do not know what you can *do* about it, consult with a music lawyer.

Your Band, Inc.

Never underestimate the power of truly making your music your business. This is necessary if you're hoping to be able to get tax breaks on your music. There are a variety of ways to do it, depending on where you're located. Some money must go into it, sometimes ranging between $150-500. However, when you consider the fact that you will be able to get some money back once tax time rolls around, it is worth having your band or music career already incorporated.

Registering Your Work

If you're creating your music and putting it into distribution, it is worth registering your work with a performer's rights group. This means that when your music gets played on the radio or is otherwise being used, you get paid for that playtime. The nicest thing about it is that you can also register other partners who worked on various songs so that royalties can easily be paid according to percentage. Of course, if your song was created solely by you, that whole payment is all yours!

Follow the Revenue

There are a few main ways that today's musicians and artists make their money; through merchandise branding and brand deals, through touring, and through the plays on their published music. While the music may be your primary focus, you also want to be able to create a continuous stream of income where possible.

The plays on music are self-explanatory. Each stream generates income, but not as much as you might like to think. Per 1000 streams, Spotify pays approximately $3.18, versus the approximate $7.83 paid out by Apple Music, and $4.02 by Amazon Music. Once upon a time, YouTube would have been the big spender to get your music onto, but monetization takes a lot more effort these days, and per 1000 views after you reach the criteria for monetization, you make approximately $0.80. This means that making a decent amount of money on any single platform will take a dedicated fanbase to stream your music regularly.

One of the ways musicians typically bring in revenue is through live performances and through touring. Depending on where you are in your journey, this might mean local clubs, community events, weddings, festivals, or large halls and stadiums. Even if you're just opening for someone else, taking the time to do live performances is a great way to keep introducing new people to your music.

As you gain traction and popularity, you can start reaching out for brand deals with various companies. Typically, most brands require anywhere between 10,000 and 30,000 to even consider sponsoring someone, but a brand deal or sponsorship can be a great way to gather funding so that you can continue working on your music. Sometimes, brands might reach out to you as well; be decisive in which brands you're willing to put your face and brand onto. Test out the products and services and be willing to dive into the fine print of how you're making your money from the deal.

Finally, there is branded merchandise. Over time, you should develop a logo or some other identifiable branding. As your fan base expands, having merchandise like t-shirts, posters, stickers, sweaters, and hats can be beneficial. Your fans wearing your branded clothing and otherwise displaying your merch can be a great way for your name to grow and reach further.

Distribution

Back in the golden age of music production, the only way you were distributing your music was by being signed by a major label or making a potentially low-quality mixtape. These days, record labels still tend to have the largest audiences and budgets to market and advertise music by new artists, but if you are not going for a record label contract, you can still do better than a low-budget cassette recording. A number of services like Distrokid, CDBaby, and Tunecore (among others) all offer distribution to all major streaming services for fairly reasonable prices.

Why do you need a distribution service though? Where a decent chunk of your revenue as a musician or producer comes from publishing your content to the masses, you need to be able to get onto the largest streaming platforms. Unfortunately, services like Spotify no longer allow an artist to upload directly to the platform in order to get paid. If you have any hope of getting paid for your music beyond YouTube and physical copy sale, getting onto these platforms requires a distributor. Be sure to look into your available distributors carefully; each of them will have differences in what exactly you're paying for, or how you pay for certain services they offer.

If you're not into the idea of paying for your distribution, YouTube still pays for streams, but only after you reach the criteria for monetization. There is also the option of paying a small monthly subscription for Soundcloud. The catch here is that you must own 100% of all aspects of the tracks you are putting out. If the free route is how you want to go, you can always look for free music aggregator services, but be incredibly thorough in looking up the information per service and compare them against each other carefully before making your choice.

CHAPTER 10

RECORD LABELS VS INDIE PRODUCTION

———◆○◆———

There was once a time when all a musician wanted was to be signed to a major record label. It seemed like the path to riches and fame, and for a while, that was true. As the climate of the music industry has evolved, we find ourselves in a position to build ourselves up with a variety of options. The nature of social media has put the good and evil of these companies in full view, leading to the increase in both indie (or independent) labels and independent artists who are carving out their paths for success.

Each of these methods has its pros and cons. Which one will be best for you depends on your goals and ideals, and exactly how much control you want to have over your work? It also depends on what your financial goals are; each path you take offers financial compensation at different rates, provided your music is selling at all.

Major Record Labels

The most well-known of all the ways of putting out music, signing onto a major record label throws you directly into the corporate world of music production (you corporate cog, you.) Jokes aside, there's a reason these labels work. In the entire world, three major labels own and run *everything:* Sony Music Entertainment, Warner Music Group, and Universal Music Group. Any other major corporate-level labels are owned under one of these groups. This comes with some distinct advantages and some profound disadvantages.

Pros

- While your indie label might know everyone in Denver, major labels are connected *all over the world.* This means an unlimited reach if you are keeping up with the numbers. These connections mean the ability to spread your music way further.

- Before you've even picked up a pen to sign your contract, the record company already knows how they're going to sell you. Especially if you're doing well within the first 6-12 months, they'll pour their focus and resources into you, because they know you are a smart investment. This means making bigger money and spreading your name further than you ever thought possible because the label is making sure to focus on what you're doing.

- Because of the international status of the three major umbrella labels, international fame is within reach when you are signed on with a major label.

- These labels don't just mean reach; they give you *status*. Having Universal, Warner, or Sony connected to your name in some way, whether directly or indirectly, means that you're more likely to hear "yes" when you're seeking to expand on your brand. If a major label has signed you, other networks and opportunities are likely to show up, because you've already proven yourself as an asset to a corporate entity that is known to be looking for an ROI. People are going to consider you a safer bet to work with if you're related to the status of such a successful organization.

- Once you're signed to a label, you now have access to the biggest names in the professional industry. This means that your team of producers, engineers, musicians, photographers, and everyone else is made up of people who are at the top of their field, which will boost the quality of your music beyond what you would ever expect to do on your own.

Cons

- Your rights are gone. Once your pen hits the paper and writes out your name, these labels own you. It is not unlike being in the military; you sign yourself away to them, they control your career, they own your work, and they send you out on tour when they feel like it.

- You only get a small portion of your sales. To be making the major money, you have to be producing *major* sales. These labels are investing in you; this means they expect a hefty ROI (Return on Investment) from your work. This also means that from your sales, a good chunk of your money is going to be used to pay everyone from the producer to the janitor.

- If you have signed to a label and you are not living up to their expected financial return, a major label will quickly turn their focus away from you and onto someone who is making them more money. You aren't their focus unless you're lining their pockets.

- Oh, did you want control over your work as a creative artist? Did you want to influence your work in a way that is authentically you? That's not going to happen with a major record label. They have already designed your packaging and created the mold that you're going to fill. Creative control doesn't live here.

Indie Labels

Indie labels, or Independent labels, are not owned by major corporations. These are people who started their own labels, typically with a decent reach within their local areas or sometimes started by musicians who have found enough success to create their own labels.

Pros

- Most indie label contracts will expire, and depending on the terms you've agreed to, many times you own your work after the contract expires. Indie labels don't exercise the same level of control that a major label does, so you can negotiate the terms of your deal, including your percentage of the money you take from your proceeds, and your tour schedule.

- You are likely going to keep a larger percentage of your sales. There are fewer people that are being paid from your sales, so depending on what you negotiate, your manner of creating music (for example, are you doing everything yourself, or are you using their engineers), and your expenses, more money lands in your account.

- Indie labels tend to take on fewer people, so when it comes time to be creating and pushing music, you're going to garner a lot more of their focus. Even if you're not taking off as fast as they'd hoped, they'll continue to put focus on you so that you're more likely to succeed.

- An indie label deciding to sign you means that they're already fans of you as an artist. While they may offer guidance, they're not designing the package they're going to sell you in. An indie label is often looking to encourage your development as an artist, versus telling you who to be.

Cons

- While it is great that you will contractually keep a larger percentage of your sales in comparison to a major label, there's a good chance you'll also be making less money in overall sales. An indie label doesn't have the reach of a major corporate label, or the budget to launch your career into the stratosphere within mere weeks to months.

Independent Artists

If you are currently putting out music without a label backing you, this is you. An independent artist is completely on their own, running their show and doing things on their schedule.

Pros

- You own 100% of your work, meaning you keep 100% of your proceeds, apart from what you pay your team for their time, service, and contribution.

- You have complete control over creative direction and scheduling. You don't want to tour right now? Cool, don't. Do you want to shift from a pop artist to a rock artist? Do it! Your career is 100% in your hands.

Cons

- When you are completely solo, you have an *extremely* limited reach. It is entirely on you to be making connections within the industry, to be seen on social media and streaming services, and to be producing content on a schedule that will keep up with your peers, while also juggling your life. This means it will take you longer to take off, but the returns on such a high-risk endeavor mean it is a way bigger pay-off when you do make it.

- Staying independent means you have to produce your own funding. This could be from your day job, taking out a loan, or any manner of ways to fund your dreams. The risk is entirely on you and your bank account.

- Even an indie label will have professionals on staff who can offer guidance if you're struggling in any area. If you're completely solo, you're having to essentially fight with yourself to improve and drive yourself forward to figure out where and how to improve.

No matter what, we all start off as independent artists before we catch the eye of indie or major labels. When you are starting, it is ideal to have your goal in mind and to know what you want to do in your music career. What level of control do you want over your music? Do you want complete control over what you're doing, or are you alright with giving up the reins to a larger entity? Your career is up to you; knowing all of these pros and cons should help you figure out what path is the best for you.

CHAPTER 11

MAKING A NAME FOR YOURSELF

---◆O◆---

There is nobody in the music industry who woke up one day, put on their "I'm famous" clothes, and made their dream happen overnight. The fact is, becoming a household name takes years of work and intense dedication. There isn't any singular path to success. Some people will work for a few years before finding their big break; others might take decades. The defining factor is how much time you dedicate, how open you are to listening to those trying to help you develop your sound, and of course, a healthy dose of luck.

Don't Quit Your Day Job

This might sound insolent, but especially before your music career starts generating a livable income, do not quit your day job. For most of us in the music industry, it crosses our minds at some point to quit our jobs to focus full-time on music; unless you are already creating a steady income with your music, do not do it. You need to make sure that you can support yourself, as well as your burgeoning career. Without having the day job funding the music, you will run your wheels flat, and the music (and your life in general) will suffer for it.

When it comes to managing your finances in general, it helps to pay close attention to the flow of your cash. Track everything that is coming in carefully, and balance it as best you can with your expenses. If you have the option of borrowing or getting equipment cheap, take that option until you can comfortably fund the brand-new equipment you have your eye on. It may become desirable to update your entire wardrobe, but there is no reason not to do it on the cheap; trade with friends or find clothes at thrift stores and on online marketplaces. Thrifting also gives you a more creative method of finding your look, so it's a 2-for-1 deal; cheap clothing, and a new look to how you brand yourself, all in one.

You should also be keeping a close eye on your receipts for anything that could be considered business-related come tax season. This will vary depending on where you live, but most times, you can claim things like equipment, software, and clothing as business expenses, given that their express purpose is to help expand your brand and your name. If the expense is intended to bring in an increased income, always set aside the receipt to be discussed with the person who may be helping you with your taxes.

Expect to Work Hard, But Maintain Balance

The expectation by most new artists is that if you spend three days focused on your music, you should also then spend three days on the business aspects of your music. This is only partially true; pursuing a music career isn't a 50/50 endeavor. If you have put in three hours on your music, three hours that day should also go into promotion and engagement, searching for opportunities, and other ways to expand on your brand and reach. We know that it's important to be creating in a consistent fashion, but that consistency highly depends on you and your current resources.

This can be overwhelming, especially in the beginning. Be prepared to reach that 100% mark but build yourself gradually. The most important thing is to pace yourself according to what is reasonable for you to personally accomplish. Give yourself a sensible amount of balance between responsibilities at home, your day job, and your music career. While it is necessary to stay in the public eye when you're trying to build your fanbase, if you can't maintain putting out a new track every week, then don't try to force yourself. Everything happens on your schedule; otherwise, you risk burning yourself out and stifling the creative flow of your music. When creativity and energy are lacking, the music suffers, and ultimately, this is how a lot of musicians burn out early on in their music careers; they simply can't keep up with their own expectations and given that they've established this expectation with their followers, it becomes a major issue in maintaining that connection with their fans.

Build Your Network

Music, like so many other professions, requires the networking to make it. It's all about who you know, and what you can make out of those professional connections. Start locally, or online, by getting to know the local musicians. Make comfortable relations with them. This can mean mutual growth for all involved as you discuss what has and hasn't worked, preferred equipment, collaborative efforts, mutual support, and learning from each other as each of you improves your skills and discovers what has been working for you.

Once you have begun making connections with local and online bands, then begin the heavy-hitting connections. Start making connections with managers, distributors, artists, and other editing pros. As you progress, you will find the areas that you excel in, as well as the points where your music suffers. Connecting with people who are skilled where you might be lacking will improve the quality of the music, and it provides positives for everyone involved; you're putting out better music, and they're gaining experience to add to their musical resume.

When building your network, look for people who might be able to become a mentor to you; look for people who have the experience that you do not have, and who are willing to teach. Having someone who will be able to guide you, especially while you're establishing yourself, can help you to avoid common mistakes. They can offer information on local people who will help you to expand your reach, or services that can help you to refine your sound and get you closer to putting out your album or even land you gigs as you build up your name and fanbase.

Play Every Show You Can

Start looking for opportunities to play in live settings. This can be at various community events, coffee houses, and local festivals. When you continuously play, not only are you developing your experience and comfort level with being in front of a crowd, but you're also extending your reach. You don't know who will be standing in the audience when you play. This could mean finding more paid opportunities, or it could mean making connections within the music community. Even an open mic night can provide valuable experience and they are fantastic for meeting with other musicians who may want to collaborate, or who may be able to point you down interesting roads leading to other possible opportunities.

With that said, the pandemic certainly hit musicians in the sweet spot by making it more difficult to gather large crowds and perform. However, it also brought out a new avenue for performance over the internet, performing on Live social media. Think of it as virtual busking. It gives you an opportunity to connect with the people who already follow you for your music. Going live on platforms such as Tiktok, Facebook, and Instagram also pushes your life out to other people who may not be followers, building your platform, and welcoming more people who may become avid listeners and tippers. You can also schedule regular performances, as well as Q&A sessions and other fun interactive sessions with your growing fanbase. When you are unable to get out on a live stage, going Live on a social platform is a great alternative.

Build Your Brand and Your Presence

Social media is a blessing and a curse; on one hand, what a convenient way to get your name out there and put your content directly into your fan's hands. On the other hand, social media means needing to regularly, almost daily, engage with your followers, create content for however many platforms you are using, and having to do so often in order to stay in the public eye. Luckily, your posts don't have to be purely music; making content that will relate to your followers and fans is a great way to engage with them. Where social media can be time-consuming, investigate apps and services that will mass publish to various platforms. Some will let you edit the post per platform, but be warned; most of these services, if not potentially all, don't currently publish to Instagram, if that's a platform you're choosing to use.

As you develop your social pages, start focusing on your brand. Who is your ideal listener? If you could target any crowd to fill a hall with at your show, which would it be? Keep this question in mind with everything you do on social; what group does your post target? Use this when you are choosing your hashtags, as well as groups you choose to join on social media. What you're looking to do is build a fanbase of people who will identify with what you have to say through your music, and people who will resonate with your message.

Your presence is not limited to posting photos on Instagram and video clips on Tiktok. Create yourself a dedicated webpage. There are lots of free options to create your website, and it gives you a centralized platform that will showcase your content; this can be linked to all your social media pages, links to new releases on various streaming platforms, updates on what you've been doing, blog posts that let people know what you're doing, tour dates (when/if you reach that point), and merchandise for your fans.

Delegate Through a Curated Team

As you progress in your music career, be ready to start delegating certain tasks. Especially once you have the cash coming in, there is no reason to continue to do absolutely everything yourself. Paying people with better know-how than yourself can drive your success and take tasks off your plate so that you can focus your energy on what matters to you the most. Develop a team; a manager who can help to curate gigs and help you to figure out when tracks should drop; an editing team who can improve your sound; and fellow musicians and vocalists who can add to the sound you've developed. There are even virtual assistants who can help you to develop your social media presence and arrange scheduled posts per week so that you can focus less on social media engagement and more on what matters to you. As you continue to develop your team, you'll be able to figure out where it is you truly excel.

Connected to this thought:

Don't Be a Diva

Seriously! There is no benefit, especially when you are still technically a "nobody", to walking with your nose in the air. It is easy for us to get wrapped up in what we are doing and fall for the mentality of *"MY raw talent is the reason we're all here."* We see ourselves producing quality and take it to heart. Do not disrespect those who are here to help you; the goal isn't solely your success, but the success of all involved. Do not give people a reason to abandon you and take their skills with them. Biting the hand that feeds you never pays off. Do not do it; you are not Beyoncé. And frankly... pretty sure even

Beyoncé isn't that mean. Nobody wants to work with an inflated ego.

CONCLUSION

Pursuing music production is easily one of the most intimidating careers moves a person might make. There is a lot that goes into it, between time, money, and sheer dedication to your craft. Just the sheer amount of competition in the field can be enough to drive some people to walk away from their dreams and passions. However, there is so much available to help you, whether it's resources to learn more so that you can improve the quality of your sound, classes where you can workshop with other people who are at your skill level or above, or people you can network with to learn more about the music industry in your local area as you move up in the music world. Inspiration is around every corner! The human experience is massive, so as long as you're creating work that you and others can relate to, there's no saying how far you can take yourself in this world.

Don't Give Up!

This is honestly the best advice that I can give you when it comes to pursuing a career in any area of music production. There are always going to be points where you start to feel like the work you've put in was for nothing or feeling like you should have made it further by now. You will come up against all kinds of people who will look at your work through a different lens, or who have a different view of what qualifies as "good music." But that is the beauty of it, beyond the technical mastering of the skills, the quality of music is subjective, and is based on many factors. When these feelings begin to catch up with you, take a moment, give yourself a break, and remember that just because one person is telling you that your music is bad, it doesn't mean that it is the end of the world or your music career.

Look for the constructive criticism that can be offered. Is someone telling you "No" because they have different tastes, or is there something in the music that can be improved? I encourage you to dig into why someone might be saying no. There's no reason to take a no personally. Even if it's a hit to your pride or ego, *take the time to ask why*. Otherwise, there is no way that you can move forward and develop as an artist, engineer, or producer. If it's simply a difference in taste, then move along to the next person, it is not a big deal. If they can offer exactly what it is that turned them off, then they've just opened up a door to you to improve on. Use rejection to your benefit and continue driving forward to pursue your goals. As I have said before, nobody wakes up in the morning and simply puts on their famous pants and "I'm a big shot" underwear. This process takes time. A lot of time, in some cases. If you can get that success you are looking for in weeks, awesome! But be prepared for it to take years; some of the biggest names in music spent years, even decades, developing their craft before they finally reached their goals.

Beyond the criticism and people telling you you-know-what-you-should-do, always appreciate those who have supported you from day one. The people who follow your social media and engage with it, the people who turn up for every show, who stream the songs you have worked on hundreds of times... are the people who are really here for you. A musician of any variety is nothing without the fans who turn up for them, so while you grow your platform and further your career, never forget those who *gave you that platform, to begin with.* They are why we succeed. They are the fundamentals behind our careers and our success, and they are why we keep creating.

Final Note from the Author

If you enjoyed this book and found it helpful, please feel free to leave a review. We appreciate knowing if we've been able to make a difference in your work, and if it has, we would love to hear from you. Thank you for trusting our knowledge and expertise. May the knowledge you have gained in this book help you to blaze your path forward, no matter what your goal may be in the music production industry.

REFERENCES

MUSIC PRODUCTION FOR BEGINNERS 2022+ EDITION: HOW TO PRODUCE MUSIC, THE EASY TO READ GUIDE FOR MUSIC PRODUCERS & SONGWRITERS

Ableton. (2019). *Music production with live and push | ableton.* Ableton.com. https://www.ableton.com/en/

Ableton. (2021). *Get started | learning music (beta).* Learningmusic.ableton.com. https://learningmusic.ableton.com/

Audio plug-in. (2021, October 21). Wikipedia. https://en.wikipedia.org/wiki/Audio_plug-in

Avid. (2021). *New subscriber deals – save up to 50% – avid.* Www.avid.com. https://www.avid.com/special-offers/holiday-2021?utm_campaign=q421_promos&utm_source=google&utm_medium=cpc&utm_term=pro%20tools&Adid=562719601578&Matchtype=e&gclid=CjoKCQiA5OuNBhCRARIsACgaiqU59zFyw3yYQJuU-ONB5p_T51dxZNcwoFliB9mYz6ADdSSUBLkkR9UaAu76EALw_wcB

Bandlab. (2015). *BandLab: Music starts here.* BandLab; BandLab. https://www.bandlab.com/products/cakewalk

Bansal, D. (2021). *Frequency response curve - an overview |
sciencedirect topics.* Www.sciencedirect.com.
https://www.sciencedirect.com/topics/engineering/fr
equency-response-
curve#:~:text=A%20frequency%2Dresponse%20curv
e%20of

Bien-Kahn, J. (2016, August 26). *Why dropping music on
friday is pivotal (hint: It's not sales).* Wired.
https://www.wired.com/2016/08/new-music-
fridays-why/

Bigand, E., Tillmann, B., Poulin-Charronnat, B., &
Manderlier, D. (2005). Repetition priming: Is music
special? *The Quarterly Journal of Experimental
Psychology Section A, 58*(8), 1347–1375.
https://doi.org/10.1080/02724980443000601

Chan, T. (2019, February 6). *8 things you need to set up your
home recording studio.* Rolling Stone.
https://www.rollingstone.com/music/music-
news/home-studio-setup-recording-how-to-790937/

Cymatics. (2021). *Cymatics.fm - the #1 site for serum presets,
samplepacks & more!* Cymatics.fm.
https://cymatics.fm/

David Miles Huber, & Runstein, R. E. (2010). *Modern
recording techniques.* Focal.

Definition of DAW. (2022). PCmag.
https://www.pcmag.com/encyclopedia/term/daw

Definition of IFPI. (2022). PCmag. https://www.pcmag.com/encyclopedia/term/ifpi

Definition of XLR connector. (2022). PCmag. https://www.pcmag.com/encyclopedia/term/xlr-connector

Ehome Recording Studio. (2019, February). *The 9 home recording studio essentials for beginners.* E-Home Recording Studio. https://ehomerecordingstudio.com/home-recording-studio-essentials/

February, B. R. (2021, August 7). *The best DAWs 2021: The best digital audio workstations for PC and Mac.* MusicRadar. https://www.musicradar.com/news/the-best-daws-the-best-music-production-software-for-pc-and-mac

FL Studio. (2022). *Homepage.* FL Studio. https://flstudio.ca/

Gerken, T. (2019, February 4). Marshmello plays live Fortnite concert. *BBC News.* https://www.bbc.com/news/blogs-trending-47116429

Hicks, M. (2019). *Audio compression basics | universal audio.* Uaudio.com. https://www.uaudio.com/blog/audio-compression-basics/

How to submit your demo to a label – Spotify for artists. (2022). Artists.spotify.com.

https://artists.spotify.com/en/blog/how-to-submit-your-demo-to-a-label

https://www.facebook.com/rorypqmusic. (2018, October 24). *Basic music theory for beginners - the complete guide | Icon Collective*. Icon Collective College of Music. https://iconcollective.edu/basic-music-theory/

"Kick drum" | definition on freemusicdictionary.com. (2022). Www.freemusicdictionary.com. https://www.freemusicdictionary.com/definition/kick-drum/

Kiddle Encyclopedia. (2021). *Pitch (music) facts for kids*. Kids.kiddle.co. https://kids.kiddle.co/Pitch_(music)

LANDR. (2020, August 7). *The 8 best free DAWs to create music*. LANDR Blog. https://blog.landr.com/best-free-daw/

Lightnote. (2021). *Basic music theory lessons - Lightnote*. Www.lightnote.co. https://www.lightnote.co/

Logic. (2021). *Logic Pro*. Apple (CA). https://www.apple.com/ca/logic-pro/

Looperman. (2021). *Download free music loops samples sounds*. Looperman. https://www.looperman.com/loops

Lumen. (2021). *Measures and time signatures | Music Appreciation*. Courses.lumenlearning.com. https://courses.lumenlearning.com/musicappreciation_with_theory/chapter/measures-and-time-

signatures/#:~:text=Measure%20is%20a%20segmen
t%20of

Mallery, S. (2012). *Holiday 2012: How to set up a room for recording and mixing.* B&H Explora. https://www.bhphotovideo.com/explora/pro-audio/tips-and-solutions/holiday-2012-how-to-set-up-a-room-for-recording-and-mixing

McDonough, M. (2019, December 27). *What is the difference between mixing and mastering? | sweetwater.* InSync. https://www.sweetwater.com/insync/what-is-the-difference-between-mixing-and-mastering/

Melodics. (2021). *Melodics - the new way to learn to play music.* Www.melodics.com. https://melodics.com/

Merriam-Webster. (2019a). *Definition of frequency.* Merriam-Webster.com. https://www.merriam-webster.com/dictionary/frequency

Merriam-Webster. (2019b). *Definition of key.* Merriam-Webster.com. https://www.merriam-webster.com/dictionary/key

Merriam-Webster. (2019c). *Definition of note.* Merriam-Webster.com. https://www.merriam-webster.com/dictionary/note

Merriam-Webster. (2019d). *Definition of octave.* Merriam-Webster.com. https://www.merriam-webster.com/dictionary/octave

Merriam-Webster. (2019e). *Definition of sound wave*. Merriam-Webster.com. https://www.merriam-webster.com/dictionary/sound%20wave

Merriam-Webster. (2019f). *Definition of tone*. Merriam-Webster.com. https://www.merriam-webster.com/dictionary/tone

Merriam-Webster. (2020a). *Definition of background noise*. Merriam-Webster.com. https://www.merriam-webster.com/dictionary/background%20noise

Merriam-Webster. (2020b). *Definition of hip hop*. Merriam-Webster.com. https://www.merriam-webster.com/dictionary/hip%20hop

Merriam-Webster. (2021a). *Merriam-Webster dictionary*. Merriam-Webster.com. https://www.merriam-webster.com/dictionary/rhythm%20and%20blues

Merriam-Webster. (2021b). *Merriam-Webster dictionary*. Merriam-Webster.com. https://www.merriam-webster.com/dictionary/snare%20drum

Merriam-Webster. (2022a). *Definition of beat*. Www.merriam-Webster.com. https://www.merriam-webster.com/dictionary/beat

Merriam-Webster. (2022b). *Definition of foley*. Www.merriam-Webster.com. https://www.merriam-webster.com/dictionary/Foley

Merriam-Webster. (2022c). *Definition of rap.* Www.merriam-Webster.com. https://www.merriam-webster.com/dictionary/rap

Merriam-Webster. (2022d). *Definition of reverb.* Www.merriam-Webster.com. https://www.merriam-webster.com/dictionary/reverb

Merriam-Webster. (2022e). *Definition of scales.* Www.merriam-Webster.com. https://www.merriam-webster.com/dictionary/scales

Merriam-Webster. (2022f). *Definition of tablature.* Www.merriam-Webster.com. https://www.merriam-webster.com/dictionary/tablature

Merriam-Webster. (2022g). *Definition of tempo.* Www.merriam-Webster.com. https://www.merriam-webster.com/dictionary/tempo

Merriam-Webster. (2022h). *Definition of treble.* Www.merriam-Webster.com. https://www.merriam-webster.com/dictionary/treble

Merriam-Webster. (2022i). *Definition of tweeter.* Www.merriam-Webster.com. https://www.merriam-webster.com/dictionary/tweeter

Merriam-Webster. (2022j). *Merriam-Webster dictionary.* Merriam-Webster.com. https://www.merriam-webster.com/dictionary/liner%20notes

MusicNotes. (2018, March 23). *How to read sheet music: Step-by-step instructions.* Musicnotes Now.

https://www.musicnotes.com/now/tips/how-to-read-sheet-music/

MusicTheory.net. (2019). *musictheory.net - lessons*. Musictheory.net. https://www.musictheory.net/lessons

New, M. (n.d.). *Michael New - YouTube*. Www.YouTube.com. Retrieved November 30, 2021, from https://www.YouTube.com/user/Rhaptapsody

Open Music Theory. (2021). *Scales and scale degrees*. Open Music Theory. http://openmusictheory.com/scales.html

Owen-Flood, M. (2019, July 4). *Why Auto-Tune is not cheating*. The Recording Studio Digest. https://medium.com/the-recording-studio-digest/why-auto-tune-is-not-cheating-3d36488dda1f

Parry, G. (2017, November 21). *How to find high-quality samples for music production (and top 4 sites)*. Audio Mentor. https://www.audiomentor.com/beginner/high-quality-samples-music-production-best-sites/

Patkar, M. (2020, May 28). *The 5 best sites to learn the basics of music theory*. MakeUseOf. https://www.makeuseof.com/tag/best-sites-learn-music-theory/

PreSonus. (2021). *Studio One*. PreSonus. https://www.presonus.com/products/studio-one/

published, T. M. team. (2021, February 10). *Free music samples: download loops, hits and multis from SampleRadar.* MusicRadar. https://www.musicradar.com/news/tech/free-music-samples-royalty-free-loops-hits-and-multis-to-download

Reason Studios. (2021). *Music production with Reason Studios.* Www.reasonstudios.com. https://www.reasonstudios.com/welcome

Rothstein, A. (2020, May 31). *What are the basics of music theory.* IPR. https://www.ipr.edu/blogs/audio-production/what-are-the-basics-of-music-theory/

Royalty free definition | law insider. (2022). Law Insider; Law Insider. https://www.lawinsider.com/dictionary/royalty-free

Russell, J. (2019, September 24). *The best free music samples and loop download sites on the web.* MusicRadar. https://www.musicradar.com/news/the-best-free-music-samples-and-loop-download-sites-on-the-web

S, B. (2019). *What is pitch in music? - definition & concept video with lesson transcript | Study.com.* Study.com. https://study.com/academy/lesson/what-is-pitch-in-music-definition-lesson-quiz.html

Search | Britannica. (2022). Www.britannica.com. https://www.britannica.com/search?query=Acoustic

Seydel, R. (2019, April 17). *How to release an album: Submit music for streaming in 10 steps.* LANDR Blog. https://blog.landr.com/how-to-release-an-album/

Shields, T. (2021, May 12). *How to find free audio samples.* Emastered.com. https://emastered.com/blog/free-audio-samples

Skelton, E. (2018, May 7). *Why does so much new music drop at the same time each friday?* Complex. https://www.complex.com/pigeons-and-planes/2018/05/why-does-so-much-music-release-friday-each-week

SoundPure. (2019, February 12). *The parts of an acoustic guitar.* Sound Pure. https://www.soundpure.com/a/expert-advice/guitars/parts-of-an-acoustic-guitar/

Splice. (2019). *Royalty-Free sounds, FX, presets & more - Splice.* Splice. https://splice.com/features/sounds

Storey, A. (2017, December 19). *What are beats per minute and what can BPM tell you? - Storyblocks Blog.* Storyblocks Blog. https://blog.storyblocks.com/tutorials/what-are-beats-per-minute-bpm/

Sweetwater. (1999, March 10). *Loop.* InSync. https://www.sweetwater.com/insync/loop-2/

Sweetwater. (2000, November 20). *Bass trap.* InSync. https://www.sweetwater.com/insync/bass-trap/

Sweetwater. (2003, June 26). *Acoustic treatment*. InSync. https://www.sweetwater.com/insync/acoustic-treatment/

What is an arrangement in music? Definition, elements & rules. (2022). Promusicianhub.com. https://promusicianhub.com/what-is-arrangement-music/

What's the difference between home stereo speakers and studio monitors? (2015). Neumann.com. https://www.neumann.com/homestudio/en/difference-between-home-stereo-speakers-and-studio-monitors

Wikipedia. (2022, January 20). *Cover art*. Wikipedia. https://en.wikipedia.org/wiki/Cover_art

Zapsplat. (2018a). *ZapSplat - download free sound effects & royalty free music*. ZapSplat - Download Free Sound Effects. https://www.zapsplat.com/

Zapsplat. (2018b). *ZapSplat - free sound effects categories*. ZapSplat - Download Free Sound Effects. https://www.zapsplat.com/sound-effect-categories/

MUSIC PRODUCTION, SONGWRITING, & AUDIO ENGINEERING, 2022+ EDITION: THE PROFESSIONAL GUIDE FOR MUSIC PRODUCERS, SONGWRITERS & AUDIO ENGINEERS IN MUSIC STUDIOS

7 Types of Acoustic Treatments. (2020, November 13).
Retrieved August 19, 2021, from Illuminated
Integration website: https://illuminated-
integration.com/blog/7-types-of-acoustic-treatments/

A Beginner's Guide to Recording
Guitar/Bass/Keyboards/Drums. (2014, November 2).
Retrieved March 25, 2021, from E-Home Recording
Studio website:
https://ehomerecordingstudio.com/recording-guitar-
bass-keyboards-drums/

Bauer, C. (2020, June 2). Indie VS Major Record Label: The
Major Differences. Retrieved September 26, 2021,
from UnifiedManufacturing website:
https://www.unifiedmanufacturing.com/blog/indie-
artist-label-artist-major-differences/

Bogomolova, P. (2021, October 26). The Pros & Cons Of
Signing With A Major Label vs. An Indie Label vs.
Staying An Independent Artist. Retrieved from
Magnetic Magazine website:
https://www.magneticmag.com/2021/10/pros-cons-
of-signing-with-major-label-vs-indie-label-vs-staying-
independent/

Briones, A. (2015, December 18). The Different Types Of
Mics And Their Uses | Gearank. Retrieved from
Gearank.com website:
https://www.gearank.com/articles/types-of-mics

Estrella, Espie. (2019). What Are the Basic Elements of Music? Retrieved from LiveAbout website: https://www.liveabout.com/the-elements-of-music-2455913

Fabry, M. (2018, May 1). What Was the First Sound Ever Recorded by a Machine? Retrieved from Time website: https://time.com/5084599/first-recorded-sound/

Ferreira, B. (2017, April 9). Listen to the Eerie Warbles of the Oldest Sound Recording in History. Retrieved from www.vice.com website: https://www.vice.com/en/article/9a7x48/listen-to-the-eerie-warbles-of-the-oldest-sound-recording-in-history

Gibson, J. (n.d.). The MIDI Standard: Introduction to MIDI and Computer Music: Center for Electronic and Computer Music: Jacobs School of Music. Retrieved from cecm.indiana.edu website: https://cecm.indiana.edu/361/midi.html#:%7E:text=MIDI%20is%20an%20acronym%20that

Gunn, N. (2016, February 11). 15 things you MUST do to make it in the music industry. Retrieved July 13, 2020, from DIY Musician Blog website: https://diymusician.cdbaby.com/music-career/15-things-must-make-music-industry/

How to Record Better Vocals: The Beginner's Guide. (2012, October 18). Retrieved May 9, 2021, from E-Home Recording Studio website: https://ehomerecordingstudio.com/recording-vocals/

How To Start A Track. (2015, December 16). Retrieved January 18, 2022, from Pheek's Mixdown and Mastering website: https://audioservices.studio/blog/music-production-tips-how-to-start-a-track

Indeed Editorial Team. (2021, February 25). How To Get Into the Music Industry | Indeed.com. Retrieved January 18, 2022, from Indeed Career Guide website: https://www.indeed.com/career-advice/finding-a-job/how-to-get-into-music-industry

Lorinczi, S. (2021, November 11). Parts of a Song - Song Structure for Songwriters. Retrieved from blog.songtrust.com website: https://blog.songtrust.com/the-parts-of-a-song

Mayes-Wright, C. (2009, December). A Beginner's Guide To Acoustic Treatment. Retrieved from Soundonsound.com website: https://www.soundonsound.com/sound-advice/beginners-guide-acoustic-treatment

Microphone Stands 101: The Ultimate Beginner's Guide. (2012, November 24). Retrieved from E-Home Recording Studio website:

https://ehomerecordingstudio.com/microphone-stands/

Murphy, C. (2019, January 8). 4 Song Structure Types You Need to Know & When to Use Them. Retrieved from Careers In Music | Music Schools & Colleges website: https://www.careersinmusic.com/song-structure/

Music Production 101: The 4 Basic Steps to Recording a Song. (2018, October). Retrieved from E-Home Recording Studio website: https://ehomerecordingstudio.com/how-to-record-a-song/

Roth, D. (2018, February 7). How to Master a Song at Home (in 14 Easy Steps). Retrieved April 20, 2021, from Musician on a Mission website: https://www.musicianonamission.com/how-to-master-a-song/

SAYANA. (2021, March 12). 8 tips for writing better lyrics. Retrieved from Splice Blog website: https://splice.com/blog/tips-writing-better-lyrics/?utm_source=google&utm_medium=cpc&utm_campaign=Google_Search_Acquisition_Sounds_Nonbrand_DSA_ROW&utm_content=sounds&utm_term=&campaignid=13577111017&adgroupid=123041963239&adid=528665014304&gclid=CjoKCQiA8vSOBhCkARIsAGdp6RS7OVob-

cXF9doqLShUhX_fW4TxQTMdUpVer6y1L3jXqgWs1
oGtyCUaApjXEALw_wcB

Stolpe, A. (2016, July 28). How to Write Song Lyrics.
Retrieved from Berklee Online Take Note website:
https://online.berklee.edu/takenote/how-to-write-
song-lyrics/

Stoubis, N. (2019, November 9). Basic Song Structure
Explained. Retrieved from Fender website:
https://www.fender.com/articles/play/parts-of-a-
song-keep-it-straight

The 9 Home Recording Studio Essentials for Beginners.
(2019, February). Retrieved March 31, 2021, from E-
Home Recording Studio website:
https://ehomerecordingstudio.com/home-recording-
studio-essentials/

The Skip. (2014, May 2). Retrieved from Music Machinery
website:
https://musicmachinery.com/2014/05/02/the-skip/

Yates, C. (2019, June 27). Scaffolding: How to Use Structure
to Map Out the Energy Flow of Your Song – Soundfly.
Retrieved from Soundfly website:
https://flypaper.soundfly.com/write/scaffolding-
song-structure/

OTHER BOOKS BY TOMMY SWINDALI

Scan the QR code with your smartphone to be taken to a truly amazing collection of books by Tommy Swindali!

DISCOVER "HOW TO FIND YOUR SOUND"

https://www.subscribepage.com/tsmusic

Scan the QR code for more.